THE MEDIEVAL LIBRARY UNDER
THE GENERAL EDITORSHIP OF
SIR ISRAEL GOLLANCZ, Litt.D., F.B.A.

THE LOVE OF BOOKS
BEING THE PHILOBIBLON
OF RICHARD DE BURY

The Seal of Richard de Bury,
Bishop of Durham.

THE LOVE OF BOOKS THE PHILOBIBLON OF RICHARD DE BURY NEWLY TRANSLATED INTO ENGLISH BY E. C. THOMAS

COOPER SQUARE PUBLISHERS, INC.
NEW YORK
1966

"TAKE THOU A BOOK INTO THINE HANDS AS SIMON THE JUST TOOK THE CHILD JESUS INTO HIS ARMS TO CARRY HIM AND KISS HIM. AND WHEN THOU HAST FINISHED READING, CLOSE THE BOOK AND GIVE THANKS FOR EVERY WORD OUT OF THE MOUTH OF GOD ; BECAUSE IN THE LORD'S FIELD THOU HAST FOUND A HIDDEN TREASURE."

THOMAS À KEMPIS : *Doctrinale Juvenum*

Published 1966 by Cooper Square Publishers, Inc.
59 Fourth Avenue, New York, N. Y. 10003
Library of Congress Catalog Card No. 66-23971

Printed in the United States of America
by Noble Offset Printers, Inc., New York, N. Y. 10003

PREFACE

The Author of the Book. Richard de Bury (1281–1345), so called from being born near Bury St. Edmunds, was the son of Sir Richard Aungerville. He studied at Oxford; and was subsequently chosen to be tutor to Prince Edward of Windsor, afterwards Edward III. His loyalty to the cause of Queen Isabella and the Prince involved him in danger. On the accession of his pupil he was made successively Cofferer, Treasurer of the Wardrobe, Archdeacon or Northampton, Prebendary of Lincoln, Sarum, and Lichfield, Keeper of the Privy Purse, Ambassador on two occasions to Pope John XXII, who appointed him a chaplain of the papal chapel, Dean of Wells, and ultimately, at the end of the year 1333, Bishop of Durham; the King and Queen, the King of Scots, and all the magnates north of the Trent, together with a multitude of nobles and many others, were present at his enthronization. It is noteworthy that during his

stay at Avignon, probably in 1330, he made the
acquaintance of Petrarch, who has left us a brief
account of their intercourse. In 1332 Richard
visited Cambridge, as one of the King's commissioners,
to inquire into the state of the King's Scholars there,
and perhaps then became a member of the Gild of St.
Mary—one of the two gilds which founded Corpus
Christi College.

In 1334 he became High Chancellor of England,
and Treasurer in 1336, resigning the former office in
1335, so that he might help the King in dealing with
affairs abroad and in Scotland, and took a most distinguished part in diplomatic negociations between
England and France. In 1339 he was again in his
bishopric. Thereafter his name occurs often among
those appointed to treat of peace with Philip of
France, and with Bruce of Scotland. It appears that
he was not in Parliament in 1344. Wasted by long
sickness—*longa infirmitate decoctus*—on the 14th of
April, 1345, Richard de Bury died at Auckland, and
was buried in Durham Cathedral.

Dominus Ricardus de Bury migravit ad Dominum.

The Bishop as Booklover. According to
the concluding note, the *Philobiblon* was completed on

the bishop's fifty-eighth birthday, the 24th of January,
1345, so that even though weakened by illness,
Richard must have been actively engaged in his
literary efforts to the very end of his generous and
noble life. His enthusiastic devoted biographer
Chambre * gives a vivid account of the bishop's book-
loving propensities, supplementary to what can be
gathered from the *Philobiblon* itself. " *Iste summe delec-
tabatur in multitudine librorum;* he had more books,
as was commonly reported, than all the other English
bishops put together. He had a separate library in
each of his residences, and wherever he was residing,
so many books lay about his bed-chamber, that it was
hardly possible to stand or move without treading
upon them. All the time he could spare from business was devoted either to religious offices or to his
books. Every day while at table he would have a
book read to him, unless some special guest were
present, and afterwards would engage in discussion on
the subject of the reading. The haughty Anthony
Bec delighted in the appendages of royalty—to be
addressed by nobles kneeling, and to be waited on in
his presence-chamber and at his table by Knights bare-

---

* *Cp.* Surtees' Society's edition of *Scriptores Tres* ; also Whar-
ton's *Anglia Sacra.*

headed and standing ; but De Bury loved to surround himself with learned scholars. Among these were such men as Thomas Bradwardine, afterwards Archbishop of Canterbury, and author of the *De Causa Dei* ; Richard Fitzralph, afterwards Archbishop of Armagh, and famous for his hostility to the mendicant orders ; Walter Burley, who dedicated to him a translation of the *Politics of Aristotle*, made at his suggestion ; John Mauduit, the astronomer ; Robert Holkot, author of many books ; Richard de Kilvington ; Richard Benworth, afterwards Bishop of London ; and Walter Seagrave, who became Dean of Chichester." *

The Bishop's Books.

In the *Philobiblon*, Richard de Bury frankly and clearly describes his means and method of collecting books. Anyhow his object was clearly not selfish. The treatise contains his rules for the library of the new College at Oxford —Durham College (where Trinity College now

---

* An unsuccessful attempt has been made to transfer the authorship of the book to Robert Holkot. Various theories have been advanced against Richard's claims. It is noteworthy that his contemporary Adam Murimuth disparages him as " *mediocriter literatus, volens tamen magnus clericus reputari,*" but such disparagement must be taken with the utmost caution. The really difficult fact to be accounted for is the omission on the part of Chambre to mention the book.

stands)—which he practically founded, though his
successor, Bishop Hatfield, carried the scheme into
effect. It is traditionally reported that Richard's
books were sent, in his lifetime or after his death, to
the house of the Durham Benedictines at Oxford, and
there remained until the dissolution of the College by
Henry VIII., when they were dispersed, some going
into Duke Humphrey's (the University) library,
others to Balliol College, and the remainder passing
into the hands of Dr. George Owen, who purchased
the site of the dissolved College.*

Unfortunately, the "special catalogue" of his
books prepared by Richard has not come down to us ;
but "from his own book and from the books cited in
the works of his friends and housemates, who may
reasonably be supposed to have drawn largely from

---

* Mr. J. W. Clark puts the matter as follows :—"Durham College, maintained by the Benedictines of Durham, was
supplied with books from the mother-house, lists of which have
been preserved ; and subsequently a library was built there to
contain the collection bequeathed in 1345 by Richard de Bury"
(*The Care of Books*, p. 142). Mr. Thomas points out that De
Bury's executors sold at least some portion of his books ; and,
moreover, his biographer says nothing of a library at Oxford.
Possibly the scheme was never carried out. In the British
Museum (Roy. 13 D. iv. 3) is a large folio MS. of the works
of John of Salisbury, which was one of the books bought back
from the Bishop's executors.

the bishop's collection, it would be possible to restore a hypothetical but not improbable *Bibliotheca Ricardi de Bury*. The difficulty would be with that contemporary literature, which they would think below the dignity of quotation, but which we know the Bishop collected."

Early Editions of the Philobiblon.

The book was first printed at Cologne in 1473, at Spires in 1483, and at Paris in 1500. The first English edition appeared in 1598–9, edited by Thomas James, Bodley's first librarian. Other editions appeared in Germany in 1610, 1614, 1674 and 1703; at Paris in 1856; at Albany in 1861. The texts were, with the exception of those issued in 1483 and 1599, based on the 1473 edition; though the French edition and translation of 1856, prepared by M. Cocheris, claimed to be a critical version, it left the text untouched, and merely gave the various readings of the three Paris manuscripts at the foot of the pages; these readings are moreover badly chosen, and the faults of the version are further to be referred to the use of the ill-printed 1703 edition as copy.

In 1832 there appeared an anonymous English translation, now known to have been by J. B. Inglis;

it followed the edition of 1473, with all its errors and inaccuracies.

Mr. E. C. Thomas' Text.—The first true text of the *Philobiblon*, the result of a careful examination of twenty-eight MSS., and of the various printed editions, appeared in the year 1888 :—

"The *Philobiblon* of Richard de Bury, Bishop of Durham, Treasurer and Chancellor of Edward III, edited and translated by Ernest C. Thomas, Barrister-at-law, late Scholar of Trinity College, Oxford, and Librarian of the Oxford Union. London : Kegan Paul, Trench, & Co."

For fifteen years the enthusiastic editor—an ideal Bibliophile—had toiled at his labour of love, and his work was on all sides received with the recognition due to his monumental achievement. To the great loss of English learning, he did not long survive the conclusion of his labours. The very limited edition of the work was soon exhausted, and it is by the most generous permission of his father, Mr. John Thomas, of Lower Broughton, Manchester, that the translation—the only trustworthy rendering of Richard de Bury's precious treatise—is now, for the first time, made accessible to the larger book-loving public, and fittingly inaugurates the present series of English classics. The general Editor desires to express his best thanks to Mr. John Thomas, as also to Messrs. Kegan Paul, for their kindness in allowing him to avail himself of the materials included in the 1888 edition of the work. He has attempted, in the brief Preface and Notes, to condense Mr. Thomas' labours in such a way as would have been acceptable to the lamented scholar, and though he has made bold to explain some few textual difficulties, and to add some few references, he would fain hope that these additions have been made with modest caution—with the reverence due to the unstinted toil of a Bibliophile after Richard de Bury's own pattern. Yet once again Richard de Bury's *Philobiblon*, edited and translated into English by E. C. Thomas, is presented to new generations of book-lovers :—

"Librorum Dilectoribus."

THE PHILOBIBLON
NEWLY TRANSLATED

PROLOGUE

TO all the faithful of Christ to whom the tenor of these presents may come, Richard de Bury, by the divine mercy Bishop of Durham, wisheth everlasting salvation in the Lord and to present continually a pious memorial of himself before God, alike in his lifetime and after his death.

What shall I render unto the Lord for all His benefits towards me ? asks the most devout Psalmist, an invincible King and first among the prophets ; in which most grateful question he approves himself a willing thank-offerer, a multifarious debtor, and one who wishes for a holier counsellor than himself : agreeing with Aristotle, the chief of philosophers, who shows (in the 3rd and 6th books of his Ethics) that all action depends upon counsel.

And indeed if so wonderful a prophet, having a fore-knowledge of divine secrets, wished so anxiously to consider how he might gratefully repay the blessings graciously bestowed, what can we fitly do, who are but rude thanksgivers and most greedy receivers, laden with infinite divine benefits ? Assuredly we ought with anxious deliberation and abundant consideration, having first invoked the Sevenfold Spirit, that it may burn in our musings as an illuminating fire, fervently to prepare a way without hinderance, that the bestower of all things may be cheerfully worshipped in return for the gifts that He has bestowed, that our neighbour may be relieved of his burden, and that the guilt contracted by sinners every day may be redeemed by the atonement of almsgiving.

Forewarned therefore through the admonition of the Psalmist's devotion by Him who alone prevents and perfects the goodwill of man, without Whom we have no power even so much as to think, and Whose gift we doubt not it is, if we have done anything good, we have diligently inquired and considered in our own heart as well as with others, what among the good offices of various works of piety would most please the Almighty, and would be more beneficial to the Church Militant. And lo ! there soon occurred to

our contemplation a host of unhappy, nay, rather of
elect scholars, in whom God the Creator and Nature
His handmaid planted the roots of excellent morals
and of famous sciences, but whom the poverty of
their circumstances so oppressed that before the frown
of adverse fortune the seeds of excellence, so fruitful
in the cultivated field of youth, not being watered by
the rain that they require, are forced to wither away.
Thus it happens that "bright virtue lurks buried in
obscurity," to use the words of Boethius, and burning
lights are not put under a bushel, but for want of oil
are utterly extinguished. Thus the field, so full of
flower in Spring, has withered up before harvest time ;
thus wheat degenerates to tares, and vines into the
wild vines, and thus olives run into the wild olive ;
the tender stems rot away altogether, and those who
might have grown up into strong pillars of the
Church, being endowed with the capacity of a subtle
intellect, abandon the schools of learning.   With
poverty only as their stepmother, they are repelled
violently from the nectared cup of philosophy as soon
as they have tasted of it and have become more fiercely
thirsty by the very taste.   Though fit for the liberal
arts and disposed to study the sacred writings alone,
being deprived of the aid of their friends, by a kind

of apostasy they return to the mechanical arts solely
to gain a livelihood, to the loss of the Church and
the degradation of the whole clergy.   Thus Mother
Church conceiving sons is compelled to miscarry, nay,
some misshapen monster is born untimely from her
womb, and for lack of that little with which Nature
is contented, she loses excellent pupils, who might
afterwards become champions and athletes of the
faith.   Alas, how suddenly the woof is cut, while the
hand of the weaver is beginning his work !   Alas,
how the sun is eclipsed in the brightness of the dawn,
and the planet in its course is hurled backwards, and,
while it bears the nature and likeness of a star suddenly drops and becomes a meteor !   What more
piteous sight can the pious man behold ?   What can
more sharply stir the bowels of his pity ?   What can
more easily melt a heart hard as an anvil into hot
tears ?   On the other hand, let us recall from past
experience how much it has profited the whole
Christian commonwealth, not indeed to enervate
students with the delights of a Sardanapalus or the
riches of a Croesus, but rather to support them in
their poverty with the frugal means that become the
scholar.   How many have we seen with our eyes,
how many have we read of in books, who, distinguished

by no pride of birth, and rejoicing in no rich inheritance, but supported only by the piety of the good,
have made their way to apostolic chairs, have most
worthily presided over faithful subjects, have bent
the necks of the proud and lofty to the ecclesiastical
yoke and have extended further the liberties of the
Church !

Accordingly, having taken a survey of human
necessities in every direction, with a view to bestow
our charity upon them, our compassionate inclina-
tions have chosen to bear pious aid to this calamitous
class of men, in whom there is nevertheless such
hope of advantage to the Church, and to provide for
them, not only in respect of things necessary to
their support, but much more in respect of
the books so useful to their studies. To this end,
most acceptable in the sight of God, our attention
has long been unweariedly devoted. This ecstatic
love has carried us away so powerfully, that we have
resigned all thoughts of other earthly things, and have
given ourselves up to a passion for acquiring books.
That our intent and purpose, therefore, may be known
to posterity as well as to our contemporaries, and that
we may for ever stop the perverse tongues of gossipers
as far as we are concerned, we have published a little

treatise written in the lightest style of the moderns ; for it is ridiculous to find a slight matter treated of in a pompous style. And this treatise (divided into twenty chapters) will clear the love we have had for books from the charge of excess, will expound the purpose of our intense devotion, and will narrate more clearly than light all the circumstances of our undertaking. And because it principally treats of the love of books, we have chosen, after the fashion of the ancient Romans, fondly to name it by a Greek word, *Philo-biblon.*

CHAPTER I

THAT THE TREASURE OF WISDOM IS CHIEFLY
CONTAINED IN BOOKS

THE desirable treasure of wisdom and science,
which all men desire by an instinct of nature,
infinitely surpasses all the riches of the world;
in respect of which precious stones are worthless;
in comparison with which silver is as clay and
pure gold is as a little sand; at whose splendour
the sun and moon are dark to look upon; compared with whose marvellous sweetness honey and
manna are bitter to the taste. O value of wisdom
that fadeth not away with time, virtue ever flourish-
ing, that cleanseth its possessor from all venom! O
heavenly gift of the divine bounty, descending from
the Father of lights, that thou mayest exalt the
rational soul to the very heavens! Thou art the

celestial nourishment of the intellect, which those who eat shall still hunger and those who drink shall still thirst, and the gladdening harmony of the languishing soul which he that hears shall never be confounded.   Thou art the moderator and rule of morals, which he who follows shall not sin.   By thee kings reign and princes decree justice.   By thee, rid of their native rudeness, their minds and tongues being polished, the thorns of vice being torn up by the roots, those men attain high places of honour, and become fathers of their country, and companions of princes, who without thee would have melted their spears into pruning-hooks and ploughshares, or would perhaps be feeding swine with the prodigal.

Where dost thou chiefly lie hidden, O most elect treasure ! and where shall thirsting souls discover thee ?

Certes, thou hast placed thy tabernacle in books, where the Most High, the Light of lights, the Book of Life, has established thee.   There everyone who asks receiveth thee, and everyone who seeks finds thee, and to everyone that knocketh boldly it is speedily opened.   Therein the cherubim spread out their wings, that the intellect of the students may ascend and look from pole to pole, from the east and west, from the north and from the south. Therein the mighty and incomprehensible God Himself is apprehensibly contained and worshipped ; therein is revealed the nature of things celestial, terrestrial, and infernal ; therein are discerned the laws by which every state is administered, the offices of the celestial hierarchy are distinguished, and the tyrannies of demons described, such as neither the ideas of Plato transcend, nor the chair of Crato contained.

In books I find the dead as if they were alive ; in books I foresee things to come ; in books warlike affairs are set forth ; from books come forth the laws of peace. All things are corrupted and decay in time ; Saturn ceases not to devour the children that he generates ; all the glory of the world would be buried in oblivion, unless God had provided mortals with the remedy of books.

Alexander, the conqueror of the earth, Julius, the invader of Rome and of the world, who, the first in war and arts, assumed universal empire under his single rule, faithful Fabricius and stern Cato, would now have been unknown to fame, if the aid of books had been wanting. Towers have been razed to the ground ; cities have been overthrown ; triumphal arches have perished from decay ; nor can either pope

or king find any means of more easily conferring the
privilege of perpetuity than by books. The book
that he has made renders its author this service in
return, that so long as the book survives its author
remains immortal and cannot die, as Ptolemy declares
in the Prologue to his Almagest : He is not dead,
he says, who has given life to science.

Who therefore will limit by anything of another
kind the price of the infinite treasure of books, from
which the scribe who is instructed bringeth forth
things new and old ? Truth that triumphs over all
things, which overcomes the king, wine, and women,
which it is reckoned holy to honour before friendship,
which is the way without turning and the life without end, which holy Boethius considers to be threefold in thought, speech, and writing, seems to remain
more usefully and to fructify to greater profit in
books. For the meaning of the voice perishes with
the sound ; truth latent in the mind is wisdom that
is hid and treasure that is not seen ; but truth which
shines forth in books desires to manifest itself to every
impressionable sense. It commends itself to the sight
when it is read, to the hearing when it is heard, and
moreover in a manner to the touch, when it suffers
itself to be transcribed, bound, corrected, and pre-

served.   The undisclosed truth of the mind, although
it is the possession of the noble soul, yet because it
lacks a companion, is not certainly known to be delightful, while neither sight nor hearing takes account
of it.   Further the truth of the voice is patent only
to the ear and eludes the sight, which reveals to us
more of the qualities of things, and linked with the
subtlest of motions begins and perishes as it were in
a breath.   But the written truth of books, not tran-
sient but permanent, plainly offers itself to be observed,
and by means of the pervious spherules of the eyes,
passing through the vestibule of perception and the
courts of imagination, enters the chamber of intellect,
taking its place in the couch of memory, where it
engenders the eternal truth of the mind.

Finally we must consider what pleasantness of
teaching there is in books, how easy, how secret !
How safely we lay bare the poverty of human ignorance to books without feeling any shame !   They are
masters who instruct us without rod or ferule, without angry words, without clothes or money.   If you
come to them they are not asleep ; if you ask and
inquire of them they do not withdraw themselves ;
they do not chide if you make mistakes ; they do not
laugh at you if you are ignorant.   O books, who alone

are liberal and free, who give to all who ask of you
and enfranchise all who serve you faithfully ! by how
many thousand types are ye commended to learned
men in the Scriptures given us by inspiration of God !
For ye are the minds of profoundest wisdom, to which
the wise man sends his son that he may dig out
treasures : Prov. ii.   Ye are the wells of living waters,
which father Abraham first digged, Isaac digged again,
and which the Philistines strive to fill up : Gen. xxvi.
Ye are indeed the most delightful ears of corn, full
of grain, to be rubbed only by apostolic hands, that
the sweetest food may be produced for hungry souls :
Matt. xii.   Ye are the golden pots in which manna
is stored, and rocks flowing with honey, nay, combs of
honey, most plenteous udders of the milk of life, garners ever full ; ye are the tree of life and the fourfold
river of Paradise, by which the human mind is
nourished, and the thirsty intellect is watered and
refreshed.   Ye are the ark of Noah and the ladder of
Jacob, and the troughs by which the young of those
who look therein are coloured ; ye are the stones
of testimony and the pitchers holding the lamps of
Gideon, the scrip of David, from which the smoothest
stones are taken for the slaying of Goliath.   Ye are
the golden vessels of the temple, the arms of the

soldiers of the Church with which to quench all the fiery darts of the wicked, fruitful olives, vines of Engadi, fig-trees that are never barren, burning lamps always to be held in readiness—and all the noblest comparisons of Scripture may be applied to books, if we choose to speak in figures.

CHAPTER II

THE DEGREE OF AFFECTION THAT IS PROPERLY
DUE TO BOOKS

SINCE the degree of affection a thing deserves depends upon the degree of its value,
and the previous chapter shows that the value
of books is unspeakable, it is quite clear to
the reader what is the probable conclusion from
this. I say probable, for in moral science we do
not insist upon demonstration, remembering that the
educated man seeks such degree of certainty as he
perceives the subject-matter will bear, as Aristotle
testifies in the first book of his Ethics. For Tully
does not appeal to Euclid, nor does Euclid rely upon
Tully. This at all events we endeavour to prove,
whether by logic or rhetoric, that all riches and all
delights whatsoever yield place to books in the

spiritual mind, wherein the Spirit which is charity
ordereth charity.   Now in the first place, because
wisdom is contained in books more than all mortals
understand, and wisdom thinks lightly of riches, as
the foregoing chapter declares.   Furthermore, Aristotle, in his Problems, determines the question, why
the ancients proposed prizes to the stronger in gymnastic and corporeal contests, but never awarded any
prize for wisdom.   This question he solves as follows :
In gymnastic exercises the prize is better and more
desirable than that for which it is bestowed ; but it
is certain that nothing is better than wisdom : wherefore no prize could be assigned for wisdom.   And
therefore neither riches nor delights are more excellent than wisdom.   Again, only the fool will deny
that friendship is to be preferred to riches, since the
wisest of men testifies this ; but the chief of philosophers honours truth before friendship, and the truth-
ful Zorobabel prefers it to all things.   Riches, then,
are less than truth.   Now truth is chiefly maintained
and contained in holy books—nay, they are written
truth itself, since by books we do not now mean the
materials of which they are made.   Wherefore riches
are less than books, especially as the most precious of
all riches are friends, as Boethius testifies in the

second book of his *Consolation ;* to whom the truth of books according to Aristotle is to be preferred. Moreover, since we know that riches first and chiefly appertain to the support of the body only, while the virtue of books is the perfection of reason, which is properly speaking the happiness of man, it appears that books to the man who uses his reason are dearer than riches. Furthermore, that by which the faith is more easily defended, more widely spread, more clearly preached, ought to be more desirable to the faithful. But this is the truth written in books, which our Saviour plainly showed, when he was about to contend stoutly against the Tempter, girding himself with the shield of truth and indeed of written truth, declaring " it is written " of what he was about to utter with his voice.

And, again, no one doubts that happiness is to be preferred to riches. But happiness consists in the operation of the noblest and diviner of the faculties that we possess—when the whole mind is occupied in contemplating the truth of wisdom, which is the most delectable of all our virtuous activities, as the prince of philosophers declares in the tenth book of the Ethics, on which account it is that philosophy is held to have wondrous pleasures in respect of purity and solidity, as he goes on to say. But the contemplation of truth is never more perfect than in books, where the act of imagination perpetuated by books does not suffer the operation of the intellect upon the truths that it has seen to suffer interruption. Wherefore books appear to be the most immediate instruments of speculative delight, and therefore Aristotle, the sun of philosophic truth, in considering the principles of choice, teaches that in itself to philosophize is more desirable than to be rich, although in certain cases, as where for instance one is in need of necessaries, it may be more desirable to be rich than to philosophize.

Moreover, since books are the aptest teachers, as the previous chapter assumes, it is fitting to bestow on them the honour and the affection that we owe to our teachers. In fine, since all men naturally desire to know, and since by means of books we can attain the knowledge of the ancients, which is to be desired beyond all riches, what man living according to nature would not feel the desire of books? And although we know that swine trample pearls under foot, the wise man will not therefore be deterred from gathering the pearls that lie before him. A library of wisdom, then, is more precious than all wealth, and all things that are desirable cannot be compared to it. Whoever therefore claims to be zealous of truth, of happiness, of wisdom or knowledge, aye, even of the faith, must needs become a lover of books.

CHAPTER III

WHAT WE ARE TO THINK OF THE PRICE IN
THE BUYING OF BOOKS

FROM what has been said we draw this
corollary welcome to us, but (as we believe)
acceptable to few : namely, that no dearness of
price ought to hinder a man from the buying of
books, if he has the money that is demanded for
them, unless it be to withstand the malice of the
seller or to await a more favourable opportunity
of buying. For if it is wisdom only that makes
the price of books, which is an infinite treasure to
mankind, and if the value of books is unspeakable,
as the premises show, how shall the bargain be shown
to be dear where an infinite good is being bought ?
Wherefore, that books are to be gladly bought and
unwillingly sold, Solomon, the sun of men, exhorts

us in the *Proverbs : Buy the truth,* he says, *and sell not wisdom.* But what we are trying to show by rhetoric or logic, let us prove by examples from history. The arch-philosopher Aristotle, whom Averroes regards as the law of Nature, bought a few books of Speusippus straightway after his death for 72,000 sesterces. Plato, before him in time, but after him in learning, bought the book of Philolaus the Pythagorean, from which he is said to have taken the *Timæus,* for 10,000 denaries, as Aulus Gellius relates in the *Noctes Atticæ.* Now Aulus Gellius relates this that the foolish may consider how wise men despise money in comparison with books. And on the other hand, that we may know that folly and pride go together, let us here relate the folly of Tarquin the Proud in despising books, as also related by Aulus Gellius. An old woman, utterly unknown, is said to have come to Tarquin the Proud, the seventh king of Rome, offering to sell nine books, in which (as she declared) sacred oracles were contained, but she asked an immense sum for them, insomuch that the king said she was mad. In anger she flung three books into the fire, and still asked the same sum for the rest. When the king refused it, again she flung three others into the fire and still asked the same price for the three

that were left.   At last, astonied beyond measure,
Tarquin was glad to pay for three books the same
price for which he might have bought nine.   The
old woman straightway disappeared, and was never
seen before or after.   These were the Sibylline books,
which the Romans consulted as a divine oracle by
some one of the Quindecemvirs, and this is believed to
have been the origin of the Quindecemvirate.   What
did this Sibyl teach the proud king by this bold deed,
except that the vessels of wisdom, holy books, exceed
all human estimation ; and, as Gregory says of the
kingdom of Heaven : They are worth all that thou
hast ?

CHAPTER IV

THE COMPLAINT OF BOOKS AGAINST THE CLERGY
ALREADY PROMOTED

A GENERATION of vipers destroying their own parent and base offspring of the ungrateful cuckoo, who when he has grown strong slays his nurse, the giver of his strength, are degenerate clerks with regard to books. Bring it again to mind and consider faithfully what ye receive through books, and ye will find that books are as it were the creators of your distinction, without which other favourers would have been wanting.

In sooth, while still untrained and helpless ye crept up to us, ye spake as children, ye thought as children, ye cried as children and begged to be made partakers of our milk. But we being straightway moved by your tears gave you the breast of grammar

to suck, which ye plied continually with teeth and
tongue, until ye lost your native barbarousness and
learned to speak with our tongues the mighty things
of God. And next we clad you with the goodly
garments of philosophy, rhetoric and dialectic, of
which we had and have a store, while ye were naked
as a tablet to be painted on. For all the household
of philosophy are clothed with garments, that the
nakedness and rawness of the intellect may be covered.
After this, providing you with the fourfold wings of
the quadrivials that ye might be winged like the
seraphs and so mount above the cherubim, we sent you
to a friend at whose door, if only ye importunately
knocked, ye might borrow the three loaves of the
Knowledge of the Trinity, in which consists the final
felicity of every sojourner below. Nay, if ye deny
that ye had these privileges, we boldly declare that ye
either lost them by your carelessness, or that through
your sloth ye spurned them when offered to you.
If these things seem but a light matter to you, we
will add yet greater things. Ye are a chosen people,
a royal priesthood, a holy race, ye are a peculiar
people chosen into the lot of God, ye are priests and
ministers of God, nay, ye are called the very Church
of God, as though the laity were not to be called

churchmen. Ye, being preferred to the laity, sing psalms and hymns in the chancel, and, serving the altar and living by the altar, make the true body of Christ, wherein God Himself has honoured you not only above the laity, but even a little higher than the angels. For to whom of His angels has He said at any time : Thou art a priest for ever after the order of Melchisedech ? Ye dispense the patrimony of the crucified one to the poor, wherein it is required of stewards that a man be found faithful. Ye are shepherds of the Lord's flock, as well in example of life as in the word of doctrine, which is bound to repay you with milk and wool.

Who are the givers of all these things, O clerks ? Is it not books ? Do ye remember therefore, we pray, how many and how great liberties and privileges are bestowed upon the clergy through us ? In truth, taught by us who are the vessels of wisdom and intellect, ye ascend the teacher's chair and are called of men Rabbi. By us ye become marvellous in the eyes of the laity, like great lights in the world, and possess the dignities of the Church according to your various stations. By us, while ye still lack the first down upon your cheeks, ye are established in your early years and bear the tonsure on your heads, while the dread sentence of the Church is heard : *Touch not mine anointed and do my prophets no harm*, and he who has rashly touched them let him forthwith by his own blow be smitten violently with the wound of an anathema. At length yielding your lives to wickedness, reaching the two paths of Pythagoras, ye choose the left branch, and going backward ye let go the lot of God which ye had first assumed, becoming companions of thieves. And thus ever going from bad to worse, dyed with theft and murder and manifold impurities, your fame and conscience stained by sins, at the bidding of justice ye are confined in manacles and fetters, and are kept to be punished by a most shameful death. Then your friend is put far away, nor is there any to mourn your lot. Peter swears that he knows not the man : the people cry to the judge : *Crucify, crucify Him ! If thou let this man go, thou art not Cæsar's friend.* Now all refuge has perished, for ye must stand before the judgment-seat, and there is no appeal, but only hanging is in store for you. While the wretched man's heart is thus filled with woe and only the sorrowing Muses bedew their cheeks with tears, in his strait is heard on every side the wailing appeal to us, and to avoid the danger of impending death he shows the slight sign of the ancient tonsure which we bestowed upon him, begging that we may be called to his aid and bear witness to the privilege bestowed upon him. Then straightway touched with pity we run to meet the prodigal son and snatch the fugitive slave from the gates of death. The book he has not forgotten is handed to him to be read, and while with lips stammering with fear he reads a few words, the power of the judge is loosed, the accuser is withdrawn, and death is put to flight. O marvellous virtue of an empiric verse! O saving antidote of dreadful ruin! O precious reading of the psalter, which for this alone deserves to be called the book of life! Let the laity undergo the judgment of the secular arm, that either sewn up in sacks they may be carried out to Neptune, or planted in the earth may fructify for Pluto, or may be offered amid the flames as a fattened holocaust to Vulcan, or at least may be hung up as a victim to Juno: while our nursling at a single reading of the book of life is handed over to the custody of the Bishop, and rigour is changed to favour, and the forum being transferred from the laity, death is routed by the clerk who is the nursling of books.

But now let us speak of the clerks who are vessels of virtue. Which of you about to preach ascends the pulpit or the rostrum without in some way consulting us ? Which of you enters the schools to teach or to dispute without relying upon our support ? First of all, it behoves you to eat the book with Ezechiel, that the belly of your memory may be sweetened within, and thus as with the panther refreshed, to whose breath all beasts and cattle long to approach, the sweet savour of the spices it has eaten may shed a perfume without. Thus our nature secretly working in our own, listeners hasten up gladly, as the load-stone draws the iron nothing loth. What an infinite host of books lie at Paris or Athens, and at the same time resound in Britain and in Rome ! In truth, while resting they yet move, and while retaining their own places they are carried about every way to the minds of listeners. Finally, by the knowledge of literature, we establish Priests, Bishops, Cardinals, and the Pope, that all things in the ecclesiastical hierarchy may be fitly disposed. For it is from books that everything of good that befalls the clerical condition takes its origin. But let this suffice : for it pains us to recall what we have bestowed upon the degenerate clergy, because whatever gifts are distributed to the ungrateful seem to be lost rather than bestowed.

Let us next dwell a little on the recital of the

wrongs with which they requite us, the contempts and cruelties of which we cannot recite an example in each kind, nay, scarcely the main classes of the several wrongs. In the first place, we are expelled by force and arms from the homes of the clergy, which are ours by hereditary right, who were used to have cells of quietness in the inner chamber, but, alas ! in these unhappy times we are altogether exiled, suffering poverty without the gates. For our places are seized now by dogs, now by hawks, now by that biped beast whose cohabitation with the clergy was forbidden of old, from which we have always taught our nurslings to flee more than from the asp and the cockatrice ; wherefore she, always jealous of the love of us, and never to be appeased, at length seeing us in some corner protected only by the web of some dead spider, with a frown abuses and reviles us with bitter words, declaring us alone of all the furniture in the house to be unnecessary, and complaining that we are useless for any household purpose, and advises that we should speedily be converted into rich caps, sendal and silk and twice-dyed purple, robes and furs, wool and linen : and, indeed, not without reason, if she could see our inmost hearts, if she had listened to our secret counsels, if she had read the book of Theophrastus or Valerius,

or only heard the twenty-fifth chapter of Ecclesiasticus
with understanding ears.

And hence it is that we have to mourn for the homes
of which we have been unjustly robbed ; and as to our
coverings, not that they have not been given to us, but
that the coverings anciently given to us have been torn
by violent hands, insomuch that our soul is bowed
down to the dust, our belly cleaveth unto the earth.
We suffer from various diseases, enduring pains in our
backs and sides ; we lie with our limbs unstrung by
palsy, and there is no man who layeth it to heart, and
no man who provides a mollifying plaster.   Our
native whiteness that was clear with light has turned
to dun and yellow, so that no leech who should see us
would doubt that we are diseased with jaundice.
Some of us are suffering from gout, as our twisted
extremities plainly show.   The smoke and dust by
which we are continuously plagued have dulled the
keenness of our visual rays, and are now infecting our
bleared eyes with ophthalmia.   Within we are devoured by the fierce gripings of our entrails, which
hungry worms cease not to gnaw, and we undergo the
corruption of the two Lazaruses, nor is there anyone
to anoint us with balm of cedar, nor to cry to us who
have been four days dead and already stink, Lazarus

come forth ! No healing drug is bound around our cruel wounds, which are so atrociously inflicted upon the innocent, and there is none to put a plaster upon our ulcers ; but ragged and shivering we are flung away into dark corners, or in tears take our place with holy Job upon his dunghill, or——too horrible to relate ——are buried in the depths of the common sewers. The cushion is withdrawn that should support our evangelical sides, which ought to have the first claim upon the incomes of the clergy, and the common necessaries of life thus be for ever provided for us, who are entrusted to their charge.

Again, we complain of another sort of injury which is too often unjustly inflicted upon our persons. We are sold for bondmen and bondwomen, and lie as hostages in taverns with no one to redeem us. We fall a prey to the cruel shambles, where we see sheep and cattle slaughtered not without pious tears, and where we die a thousand times from such terrors as might frighten even the brave. We are handed over to Jews, Saracens, heretics and infidels, whose poison we always dread above everything, and by whom it is well known that some of our parents have been infected with pestiferous venom. In sooth, we who should be treated as masters in the sciences, and bear rule over the mechanics who should be subject to us, are instead handed over to the government of subordinates, as though some supremely noble monarch should be trodden under foot by rustic heels. Any seamster or cobbler or tailor or artificer of any trade keeps us shut up in prison for the luxurious and wanton pleasures of the clergy.

Now we would pursue a new kind of injury by which we suffer alike in person and in fame, the dearest thing we have. Our purity of race is diminished every day, while new authors' names are imposed upon us by worthless compilers, translators, and transformers, and losing our ancient nobility, while we are reborn in successive generations, we become wholly degenerate ; and thus against our will the name of some wretched stepfather is affixed to us, and the sons are robbed of the names of their true fathers. The verses of Virgil, while he was yet living, were claimed by an impostor ; and a certain Fidentinus mendaciously usurped the works of Martial, whom Martial thus deservedly rebuked :

> " The book you read is, Fidentinus ! mine,
> Though read so badly, 't well may pass for thine ! "

What marvel, then, if when our authors are dead clerical apes use us to make broad their phylacteries, since even while they are alive they try to seize us as soon as we are published ? Ah ! how often ye pretend that we who are ancient are but lately born, and try to pass us off as sons who are really fathers, calling us who have made you clerks the production of your studies. Indeed, we derived our origin from Athens, though we are now supposed to be from Rome ; for Carmentis was always the pilferer of Cadmus, and we who were but lately born in England, will to-morrow be born again in Paris ; and thence being carried to Bologna, will obtain an Italian origin, based upon no affinity of blood. Alas ! how ye commit us to treacherous copyists to be written, how corruptly ye read us and kill us by medication, while ye supposed ye were correcting us with pious zeal. Oftentimes we have to endure barbarous interpreters, and those who are ignorant of foreign idioms presume to translate us from one language into another ; and thus all propriety of speech is lost and our sense is shamefully mutilated contrary to the meaning of the author ! Truly noble would have been the condition of books if it had not been for the presumption of the tower of Babel, if but one kind of speech had been transmitted by the whole human race.

We will add the last clause of our long lament, though far too short for the materials that we have. For in us the natural use is changed to that which is against nature, while we who are the light of faithful souls everywhere fall a prey to painters knowing nought of letters, and are entrusted to goldsmiths to become, as though we were not sacred vessels of wisdom, repositories of gold-leaf. We fall undeservedly into the power of laymen, which is more bitter to us than any death, since they have sold our people for nought, and our enemies themselves are our judges.

It is clear from what we have said what infinite invectives we could hurl against the clergy, if we did not think of our own reputation. For the soldier whose campaigns are over venerates his shield and arms, and grateful Corydon shows regard for his decaying team, harrow, flail and mattock, and every manual artificer for the instruments of his craft ; it is only the ungrateful cleric who despises and neglects those things which have ever been the foundation of his honours.

CHAPTER V

THE COMPLAINT OF BOOKS AGAINST THE POSSESSIONERS

THE venerable devotion of the religious orders is wont to be solicitous in the care of books and to delight in their society, as if they were the only riches. For some used to write them with their own hands between the hours of prayer, and gave to the making of books such intervals as they could secure and the times appointed for the recreation of the body. By whose labours there are resplendent to-day in most monasteries these sacred treasuries full of cherubic letters, for giving the knowledge of salvation to the student and a delectable light to the paths of the laity. O manual toil, happier than any agricultural task ! O devout solicitude, where neither Martha nor Mary deserves to be rebuked ! O joyful house, in which the fruitful Leah does not envy the beauteous Rachel, but action and contemplation share each other's joys ! O happy charge, destined to benefit endless generations of posterity, with which no planting of trees, no sowing of seeds, no pastoral delight in herds, no building of fortified camps can be compared ! Wherefore the memory of those fathers should be immortal, who delighted only in the treasures of wisdom, who most laboriously provided shining lamps against future darkness, and against hunger of hearing the Word of God, most carefully prepared, not bread baked in the ashes, nor of barley, nor musty, but unleavened loaves made of the finest wheat of divine wisdom, with which hungry souls might be joyfully fed. These men were the stoutest champions of the Christian army, who defended our weakness by their most valiant arms ; they were in their time the most cunning takers of foxes, who have left us their nets, that we might catch the young foxes, who cease not to devour the growing vines. Of a truth, noble fathers, worthy of perpetual benediction, ye would have been deservedly happy, if ye had been allowed to beget offspring like yourselves, and to leave no degenerate or doubtful progeny for the benefit of future times.

But, painful to relate, now slothful Thersites
handles the arms of Achilles and the choice trappings
of war-horses are spread upon lazy asses, winking owls
lord it in the eagle's nest, and the cowardly kite sits
upon the perch of the hawk.

> Liber Bacchus is ever loved,
> And is into their bellies shoved,
>   By day and by night ;
> Liber Codex is neglected,
> And with scornful hand rejected,
>   Far out of their sight.

And as if the simple monastic folk of modern times
were deceived by a confusion of names, while *Liber
Pater* is preferred to *Liber Patrum*, the study of the
monks nowadays is in the emptying of cups and not
the emending of books ; to which they do not hesitate to add the wanton music of Timotheus, jealous of
chastity, and thus the song of the merry-maker and
not the chant of the mourner is become the office of
the monks.   Flocks and fleeces, crops and granaries,
leeks and potherbs, drink and goblets, are nowadays
the reading and study of the monks, except a few
elect ones, in whom lingers not the image but some
slight vestige of the fathers that preceded them.   And
again, no materials at all are furnished us to commend

the canons regular for their care or study of us, who though they bear their name of honour from their twofold rule, yet have neglected the notable clause of Augustine's rule, in which we are commended to his clergy in these words : *Let books be asked for each day at a given hour ; he who asks for them after the hour is not to receive them.* Scarcely anyone observes this devout rule of study after saying the prayers of the Church, but to care for the things of this world and to look at the plough that has been left is reckoned the highest wisdom. They take up bow and quiver, embrace arms and shield, devote the tribute of alms to dogs and not to the poor, become the slaves of dice and draughts, and of all such things as we are wont to forbid even to the secular clergy, so that we need not marvel if they disdain to look upon us, whom they see so much opposed to their mode of life.

Come then, reverend fathers, deign to recall your fathers and devote yourselves more faithfully to the study of holy books, without which all religion will stagger, without which the virtue of devotion will dry up like a sherd, and without which ye can afford no light to the world.

CHAPTER VI

THE COMPLAINT OF BOOKS AGAINST THE MENDICANTS

POOR in spirit, but most rich in faith, off-scourings of the world and salt of the earth, despisers of the world and fishers of men, how happy are ye, if suffering penury for Christ ye know how to possess your souls in patience! For it is not want the avenger of iniquity, nor the adverse fortune of your parents, nor violent necessity that has thus oppressed you with beggary, but a devout will and Christ-like election, by which ye have chosen that life as the best, which God Almighty made man as well by word as by example declared to be the best. In truth, ye are the latest offspring of the ever-fruitful Church, of late divinely substituted for the Fathers and the Prophets, that your sound may go forth into all the earth, and that instructed by our healthful doctrines ye may preach before all kings and nations the invincible faith of Christ. Moreover, that the faith of the Fathers is chiefly enshrined in books the second chapter has sufficiently shown, from which it is clearer than light that ye ought to be zealous lovers of books above all other Christians. Ye are commanded to sow upon all waters, because the Most High is no respecter of persons, nor does the Most Holy desire the death of sinners, who offered Himself to die for them, but desires to heal the contrite in heart, to raise the fallen, and to correct the perverse in the spirit of lenity. For which most salutary purpose our kindly Mother Church has planted you freely, and having planted has watered you with favours, and having watered you has established you with privileges, that ye may be co-workers with pastors and curates in procuring the salvation of faithful souls. Wherefore, that the order of Preachers was principally instituted for the study of the Holy Scriptures and the salvation of their neighbours, is declared by their constitutions, so that not only from the rule of Bishop Augustine, which directs books to be asked for every day, but as soon as they have read the prologue of the said constitutions they may know from the very title of the same that they are pledged to the love of books.

But alas ! a threefold care of superfluities, viz., of the stomach, of dress, and of houses, has seduced these men and others following their example from the paternal care of books, and from their study. For, forgetting the providence of the Saviour (who is declared by the Psalmist to think upon the poor and needy), they are occupied with the wants of the perishing body, that their feasts may be splendid and their garments luxurious, against the rule, and the fabrics of their buildings, like the battlements of castles, carried to a height imcompatible with poverty. Because of these three things, we books, who have ever procured their advancement and have granted them to sit among the powerful and noble, are put far from their heart's affection and are reckoned as superfluities ; except that they rely upon some treatises of small value, from which they derive strange heresies and apocryphal imbecilities, not for the refreshment of souls, but rather for tickling the ears of the listeners. The Holy Scripture is not expounded, but is neglected and treated as though it were commonplace and known to all, though very

few have touched its hem, and though its depth is
such, as Holy Augustine declares, that it cannot be
understood by the human intellect, however long it
may toil with the utmost intensity of study.   From
this he who devotes himself to it assiduously, if only
He will vouchsafe to open the door who has established the spirit of piety, may unfold a thousand
lessons of moral teaching, which will flourish with
the freshest novelty and will cherish the intelligence
of the listeners with the most delightful savours.
Wherefore the first professors of evangelical poverty,
after some slight homage paid to secular science, collecting all their force of intellect, devoted themselves
to labours upon the sacred scripture, meditating day
and night on the law of the Lord.   And whatever
they could steal from their famishing belly, or inter-
cept from their half-covered body, they thought it
the highest gain to spend in buying or correcting
books.   Whose worldly contemporaries observing
their devotion and study bestowed upon them for
the edification of the whole Church the books which
they had collected at great expense in the various
parts of the world.

In truth, in these days as ye are engaged with all
diligence in pursuit of gain, it may be reasonably

believed, if we speak according to human notions, that God thinks less upon those whom He perceives to distrust His promises, putting their hope in human providence, not considering the raven, nor the lilies, whom the Most High feeds and arrays. Ye do not think upon Daniel and the bearer of the mess of boiled pottage, nor recollect Elijah who was delivered from hunger once in the desert by angels, again in the torrent by ravens, and again in Sarepta by the widow, through the divine bounty, which gives to all flesh their meat in due season. Ye descend (as we fear) by a wretched anticlimax, distrust of the divine goodness producing reliance upon your own prudence, and reliance upon your own prudence begetting anxiety about worldly things, and excessive anxiety about worldly things taking away the love as well as the study of books ; and thus poverty in these days is abused to the injury of the Word of God, which ye have chosen only for profit's sake.

With summer fruit, as the people gossip, ye attract boys to religion, whom when they have taken the vows ye do not instruct by fear and force, as their age requires, but allow them to devote themselves to begging expeditions, and suffer them to spend the time, in which they might be learning, in procuring

the favour of friends, to the annoyance of their
parents, the danger of the boys, and the detriment of
the order.   And thus no doubt it happens that those
who were not compelled to learn as unwilling boys,
when they grow up presume to teach though utterly
unworthy and unlearned, and a small error in the beginning becomes a very great one in the end.   For
there grows up among your promiscuous flock of
laity a pestilent multitude of creatures, who nevertheless the more shamelessly force themselves into the
office of preaching, the less they understand what they
are saying, to the contempt of the Divine Word and
the injury of souls.   In truth, against the law ye
plough with an ox and an ass together, in committing
the cultivation of the Lord's field to learned and unlearned.   Side by side, it is written, the oxen were
ploughing and the asses feeding beside them : since
it is the duty of the discreet to preach, but of the
simple to feed themselves in silence by the hearing of
sacred eloquence.   How many stones ye fling upon
the heap of Mercury nowadays !   How many mar-
riages ye procure for the eunuchs of wisdom !   How
many blind watchmen ye bid go round about the
walls of the Church !

O idle fishermen, using only the nets of others,

which when torn it is all ye can do to clumsily repair,
but can net no new ones of your own ! ye enter on
the labours of others, ye repeat the lessons of others,
ye mouth with theatric effort the superficially repeated
wisdom of others. As the silly parrot imitates the
words that he has heard, so such men are mere re-
citers of all, but authors of nothing, imitating Balaam's
ass, which, though senseless of itself, yet became eloquent of speech and the teacher of its master though
a prophet. Recover yourselves, O poor in Christ,
and studiously regard us books, without which ye can
never be properly shod in the preparation of the
Gospel of Peace.

Paul the Apostle, preacher of the truth and excellent teacher of the nations, for all his gear bade three
things to be brought to him by Timothy, his cloak,
books and parchments, affording an example to
ecclesiastics that they should wear dress in moderation,
and should have books for aid in study, and parchments, which the Apostle especially esteems, for
writing : *and especially*, he says, the parchments.
And truly that clerk is crippled and maimed to his
disablement in many ways, who is entirely ignorant
of the art of writing. He beats the air with words
and edifies only those who are present, but does

nothing for the absent and for posterity. The man bore a writer's ink-horn upon his loins, who set a mark *Tau* upon the foreheads of the men that sigh and cry, *Ezechiel* ix. ; teaching in a figure that if any lack skill in writing, he shall not undertake the task of preaching repentance.

Finally, in conclusion of the present chapter, books implore of you : make your young men who though ignorant are apt of intellect apply themselves to study, furnishing them with necessaries, that ye may teach them not only goodness but discipline and science, may terrify them by blows, charm them by blandishments, mollify them by gifts, and urge them on by painful rigour, so that they may become at once Socratics in morals and Peripatetics in learning. Yesterday, as it were at the eleventh hour, the prudent householder introduced you into his vineyard. Repent of idleness before it is too late : would that with the cunning steward ye might be ashamed of begging so shamelessly ; for then no doubt ye would devote yourselves more assiduously to us books and to study.

CHAPTER VII

THE COMPLAINT OF BOOKS AGAINST WARS

ALMIGHTY Author and Lover of peace, scatter the nations that delight in war, which is above all plagues injurious to books. For wars being without the control of reason make a wild assault on everything they come across, and, lacking the check of reason they push on without discretion or distinction to destroy the vessels of reason. Then the wise Apollo becomes the Python's prey, and Phronesis, the pious mother, becomes subject to the power of Phrenzy. Then winged Pegasus is shut up in the stall of Corydon, and eloquent Mercury is strangled. Then wise Pallas is struck down by the dagger of error, and the charming Pierides are smitten by the truculent tyranny of madness. O cruel spectacle ! where you

may see the Phœbus of philosophers, the all-wise
Aristotle, whom God Himself made master of the
master of the world, enchained by wicked hands and
borne in shameful irons on the shoulders of gladiators
from his sacred home. There you may see him who
was worthy to be lawgiver to the lawgiver of the
world and to hold empire over its emperor, made the
slave of vile buffoons by the most unrighteous laws of
war. O most wicked power of darkness, which does
not fear to undo the approved divinity of Plato, who
alone was worthy to submit to the view of the
Creator, before he assuaged the strife of warring chaos,
and before form had put on its garb of matter, the
ideal types, in order to demonstrate the archetypal
universe to its author, so that the world of sense
might be modelled after the supernal pattern. O
tearful sight ! where the moral Socrates, whose acts
were virtue and whose discourse was science, who
deduced political justice from the principles of
nature, is seen enslaved to some rascal robber. We
bemoan Pythagoras, the parent of harmony, as,
brutally scourged by the harrying furies of war, he
utters not a song but the wailings of a dove. We
mourn, too, for Zeno, who lest he should betray his
secret bit off his tongue and fearlessly spat it out at

the tyrant, and now, alas ! is brayed and crushed to
death in a mortar by Diomedon.

In sooth we cannot mourn with the grief that they
deserve all the various books that have perished by
the fate of war in various parts of the world. Yet we
must tearfully recount the dreadful ruin which was
caused in Egypt by the auxiliaries in the Alexandrian
war, when seven hundred thousand volumes were consumed by fire. These volumes had been collected by
the royal Ptolemies through long periods of time, as
Aulus Gellius relates. What an Atlantean progeny
must be supposed to have then perished : including
the motions of the spheres, all the conjunctions of the
planets, the nature of the galaxy, and the prognostic
generations of comets, and all that exists in the
heavens or in the ether ! Who would not shudder
at such a hapless holocaust, where ink is offered up
instead of blood, where the glowing ashes of crackling
parchment were encarnadined with blood, where the
devouring flames consumed so many thousands of
innocents in whose mouth was no guile, where the
unsparing fire turned into stinking ashes so many
shrines of eternal truth ! A lesser crime than this
is the sacrifice of Jephthah or Agamemnon, where
a pious daughter is slain by a father's sword. How

many labours of the famous Hercules shall we suppose then perished, who because of his knowledge of astronomy is said to have sustained the heaven on his unyielding neck, when Hercules was now for the second time cast into the flames. The secrets of the heavens, which Jonithus learnt not from man or through man but received by divine inspiration ; what his brother Zoroaster, the servant of unclean spirits, taught the Bactrians ; what holy Enoch, the prefect of Paradise, prophesied before he was taken from the world, and finally, what the first Adam taught his children of the things to come, which he had seen when caught up in an ecstasy in the book of eternity, are believed to have perished in those horrid flames. The religion of the Egyptians, which the book of the Perfect Word so commends ; the excellent polity of the older Athens, which preceded by nine thousand years the Athens of Greece ; the charms of the Chaldæans ; the observations of the Arabs and Indians ; the ceremonies of the Jews ; the architecture of the Babylonians ; the agriculture of Noah ; the magic arts of Moses ; the geometry of Joshua ; the enigmas of Samson ; the problems of Solomon from the cedar of Lebanon to the hyssop ; the antidotes of Aesculapius ; the grammar of Cadmus ; the

poems of Parnassus ; the oracles of Apollo ; the argo-
nautics of Jason ; the stratagems of Palamedes, and
infinite other secrets of science are believed to have
perished at the time of this conflagration.

Nay, Aristotle would not have missed the quad-
rature of the circle, if only baleful conflicts had spared
the books of the ancients, who knew all the methods
of nature.   He would not have left the problem of
the eternity of the world an open question, nor, as is
credibly conceived, would he have had any doubts of
the plurality of human intellects and of their eternity,
if the perfect sciences of the ancients had not been
exposed to the calamities of hateful wars.   For by
wars we are scattered into foreign lands, are mutilated,
wounded, and shamefully disfigured, are buried under
the earth and overwhelmed in the sea, are devoured
by the flames and destroyed by every kind of death.
How much of our blood was shed by warlike Scipio,
when he was eagerly compassing the overthrow of
Carthage, the opponent and rival of the Roman
empire !   How many thousands of thousands of us
did the ten years' war of Troy dismiss from the light
of day !   How many were driven by Anthony, after
the murder of Tully, to seek hiding places in foreign
provinces !   How many of us were scattered by

Theodoric, while Boethius was in exile, into the different quarters of the world, like sheep whose shepherd has been struck down ! How many, when Seneca fell a victim to the cruelty of Nero, and willing yet unwilling passed the gates of death, took leave of him and retired in tears, not even knowing in what quarter to seek for shelter !

Happy was that translation of books which Xerxes is said to have made to Persia from Athens, and which Seleucus brought back again from Persia to Athens. O glad and joyful return ! O wondrous joy, which you might then see in Athens, when the mother went in triumph to meet her progeny, and again showed the chambers in which they had been nursed to her now aging children ! Their old homes were restored to their former inmates, and forthwith boards of cedar with shelves and beams of gopher wood are most skilfully planed ; inscriptions of gold and ivory are designed for the several compartments, to which the volumes themselves are reverently brought and pleasantly arranged, so that no one hinders the entrance of another or injures its brother by excessive crowding.

But in truth infinite are the losses which have been inflicted upon the race of books by wars and tumults. And as it is by no means possible to enumerate and survey infinity, we will here finally set up the Gades of our complaint, and turn again to the prayers with which we began, humbly imploring that the Ruler of Olympus and the Most High Governor of all the world will establish peace and dispel wars and make our days tranquil under His protection.

CHAPTER VIII

OF THE NUMEROUS OPPORTUNITIES WE HAVE
HAD OF COLLECTING A STORE OF BOOKS

SINCE to everything there is a season and an opportunity, as the wise Ecclesiastes witnesseth, let us now proceed to relate the manifold opportunities through which we have been assisted by the divine goodness in the acquisition of books.

Although from our youth upwards we had always delighted in holding social commune with learned men and lovers of books, yet when we prospered in the world and made acquaintance with the King's majesty and were received into his household, we obtained ampler facilities for visiting everywhere as we would, and of hunting as it were certain most choice preserves, libraries private as well as public, and of the regular

as well as of the secular clergy. And indeed while
we filled various offices to the victorious Prince and
splendidly triumphant King of England, Edward the
Third from the Conquest—whose reign may the
Almighty long and peacefully continue—first those
about his court, but then those concerning the public
affairs of his kingdom, namely the offices of Chancellor
and Treasurer, there was afforded to us, in consideration of the royal favour, easy access for the purpose of
freely searching the retreats of books. In fact, the
fame of our love of them had been soon winged abroad
everywhere, and we were reported to burn with such
desire for books, and especially old ones, that it was
more easy for any man to gain our favour by means
of books than of money. Wherefore, since supported
by the goodness of the aforesaid prince of worthy
memory, we were able to requite a man well or ill, to
benefit or injure mightily great as well as small, there
flowed in, instead of presents and guerdons, and instead of gifts and jewels, soiled tracts and battered
codices, gladsome alike to our eye and heart. Then
the aumbries of the most famous monasteries were
thrown open, cases were unlocked and caskets were
undone, and volumes that had slumbered through
long ages in their tombs wake up and are astonished,

and those that had lain hidden in dark places are bathed in the ray of unwonted light. These long lifeless books, once most dainty, but now become corrupt and loathsome, covered with litters of mice and pierced with the gnawings of the worms, and who were once clothed in purple and fine linen, now lying in sackcloth and ashes, given up to oblivion, seemed to have become habitations of the moth. Natheless among these, seizing the opportunity, we would sit down with more delight than a fastidious physician among his stores of gums and spices, and there we found the object and the stimulus of our affections. Thus the sacred vessels of learning came into our control and stewardship ; some by gift, others by purchase, and some lent to us for a season.

No wonder that when people saw that we were contented with gifts of this kind, they were anxious of their own accord to minister to our needs with those things that they were more willing to dispense with than the things they secured by ministering to our service. And in good will we strove so to forward their affairs that gain accrued to them, while justice suffered no disparagement. Indeed, if we had loved gold and silver goblets, high-bred horses, or no small sums of money, we might in those days have furnished

forth a rich treasury.   But in truth we wanted manuscripts not moneyscripts ; we loved codices more than
florins, and preferred slender pamphlets to pampered
palfreys.

Besides all this, we were frequently made ambassador of this most illustrious Prince of everlasting
memory, and were sent on the most various affairs of
state, now to the Holy See, now to the Court of
France, and again to various powers of the world, on
tedious embassies and in times of danger, always
carrying with us, however, that love of books which
many waters could not quench.   For this like a delicious draught sweetened the bitterness of our jour-
neyings and after the perplexing intricacies and
troublesome difficulties of causes, and the all but inex-
tricable labyrinths of public affairs afforded us a little
breathing space to enjoy a balmier atmosphere.

O Holy God of gods in Sion, what a mighty
stream of pleasure made glad our hearts whenever we
had leisure to visit Paris, the Paradise of the world,
and to linger there ; where the days seemed ever few
for the greatness of our love !   There are delightful
libraries, more aromatic than stores of spicery ; there
are luxuriant parks of all manner of volumes ; there
are Academic meads shaken by the tramp of scholars ;

there are lounges of Athens ; walks of the Peripatetics ; peaks of Parnassus ; and porches of the Stoics. There is seen the surveyor of all arts and sciences Aristotle, to whom belongs all that is most excellent in doctrine, so far as relates to this passing sublunary world ; there Ptolemy measures epicycles and eccentric apogees and the nodes of the planets by figures and numbers ; there Paul reveals the mysteries ; there his neighbour Dionysius arranges and distinguishes the hierarchies ; there the virgin Carmentis reproduces in Latin characters all that Cadmus collected in Phœnician letters ; there indeed opening our treasuries and unfastening our purse-strings we scattered money with joyous heart and purchased inestimable books with mud and sand. It is naught, it is naught, saith every buyer. But in vain ; for behold how good and how pleasant it is to gather together the arms of the clerical warfare, that we may have the means to crush the attacks of heretics, if they arise.

Further, we are aware that we obtained most excellent opportunities of collecting in the following way. From our early years we attached to our society with the most exquisite solicitude and discarding all partiality all such masters and scholars and professors in the several faculties as had become most distinguished by

their subtlety of mind and the fame of their learning.
Deriving consolation from their sympathetic conversation, we were delightfully entertained, now by demon-
strative chains of reasoning, now by the recital of
physical processes and the treatises of the doctors of
the Church, now by stimulating discourses on the
allegorical meanings of things, as by a rich and well-
varied intellectual feast.   Such men we chose as
comrades in our years of learning, as companions in
our chamber, as associates on our journeys, as guests
at our table, and, in short, as helpmates in all the
vicissitudes of life.   But as no happiness is permitted
to endure for long, we were sometimes deprived of
the bodily companionship of some of these shining
lights, when justice looking down from heaven, the
ecclesiastical preferments and dignities that they deserved fell to their portion.   And thus it happened,
as was only right, that in attending to their own cures
they were obliged to absent themselves from attend-
ance upon us.

We will add yet another very convenient way by
which a great multitude of books old as well as new
came into our hands.   For we never regarded with
disdain or disgust the poverty of the mendicant orders,
adopted for the sake of Christ ; but in all parts of the

world took them into the kindly arms of our compassion, allured them by the most friendly familiarity into devotion to ourselves, and having so allured them cherished them with munificent liberality of beneficence for the sake of God, becoming benefactors of all of them in general in such wise that we seemed none the less to have adopted certain individuals with a special fatherly affection. To these men we were as a refuge in every case of need, and never refused to them the shelter of our favour, wherefore we deserved to find them most special furtherers of our wishes and promoters thereof in act and deed, who compassing land and sea, traversing the circuit of the world, and ransacking the universities and high schools of various provinces, were zealous in combatting for our desires, in the sure and certain hope of reward. What leveret could escape amidst so many keen-sighted hunters ? What little fish could evade in turn their hooks and nets and snares ? From the body of the Sacred Law down to the booklet containing the fallacies of yesterday, nothing could escape these searchers. Was some devout discourse uttered at the fountain-head of Christian faith, the holy Roman Curia, or was some strange question ventilated with novel arguments ; did the solidity of Paris, which is now more zealous in the study of antiquity than in the subtle investigation of truth, did English subtlety, which illumined by the lights of former times is always sending forth fresh rays of truth, produce anything to the advancement of science or the declaration of the faith, this was instantly poured still fresh into our ears, ungarbled by any babbler, unmutilated by any trifler, but passing straight from the purest of wine-presses into the vats of our memory to be clarified.

But whenever it happened that we turned aside to the cities and places where the mendicants we have mentioned had their convents, we did not disdain to visit their libraries and any other repositories of books ; nay, there we found heaped up amid the utmost poverty the utmost riches of wisdom. We discovered in their fardels and baskets not only crumbs falling from the masters' table for the dogs, but the shewbread without leaven and the bread of angels having in it all that is delicious ; and indeed the garners of Joseph full of corn, and all the spoil of the Egyptians, and the very precious gifts which Queen Sheba brought to Solomon.

These men are as ants ever preparing their meat in the summer, and ingenious bees continually fabricat-

ing cells of honey. They are successors of Bezaleel
in devising all manner of workmanship in silver and
gold and precious stones for decorating the temple of
the Church. They are cunning embroiderers, who
fashion the breastplate and ephod of the high priest
and all the various vestments of the priests. They
fashion the curtains of linen and hair and coverings of
ram's skins dyed red with which to adorn the tabernacle of the Church militant. They are husband-
men that sow, oxen treading out corn, sounding
trumpets, shining Pleiades and stars remaining in
their courses, which cease not to fight against Sisera.
And to pay due regard to truth, without prejudice to
the judgment of any, although they lately at the
eleventh hour have entered the lord's vineyard, as the
books that are so fond of us eagerly declared in our
sixth chapter, they have added more in this brief
hour to the stock of the sacred books than all the
other vine-dressers; following in the footsteps of
Paul, the last to be called but the first in preaching,
who spread the gospel of Christ more widely than all
others. Of these men, when we were raised to the
episcopate we had several of both orders, viz., the
Preachers and Minors, as personal attendants and
companions at our board, men distinguished no less

in letters than in morals, who devoted themselves
with unwearied zeal to the correction, exposition,
tabulation, and compilation of various volumes.   But
although we have acquired a very numerous store of
ancient as well as modern works by the manifold in-
termediation of the religious, yet we must laud the
Preachers with special praise, in that we have found
them above all the religious most freely communica-
tive of their stores without jealousy, and proved them
to be imbued with an almost Divine liberality, not
greedy but fitting possessors of luminous wisdom.

Besides all the opportunities mentioned above, we
secured the acquaintance of stationers and booksellers,
not only within our own country, but of those spread
over the realms of France, Germany, and Italy, money
flying forth in abundance to anticipate their demands ;
nor were they hindered by any distance or by the
fury of the seas, or by the lack of means for their
expenses, from sending or bringing to us the books
that we required.   For they well knew that their
expectations of our bounty would not be defrauded,
but that ample repayment with usury was to be found
with us.

Nor, finally, did our good fellowship, which aimed
to captivate the affection of all, overlook the rectors

of schools and the instructors of rude boys. But
rather, when we had an opportunity, we entered
their little plots and gardens and gathered sweet-
smelling flowers from the surface and dug up their
roots, obsolete indeed, but still useful to the student,
which might, when their rank barbarism was digested
heal the pectoral arteries with the gift of eloquence.
Amongst the mass of these things we found some
greatly meriting to be restored, which when skilfully
cleansed and freed from the disfiguring rust of age,
deserved to be renovated into comeliness of aspect.
And applying in full measure the necessary means, as
a type of the resurrection to come, we resuscitated
them and restored them again to new life and health.

Moreover, we had always in our different manors
no small multitude of copyists and scribes, of binders,
correctors, illuminators, and generally of all who could
usefully labour in the service of books. Finally, all
of both sexes and of every rank or position who had
any kind of association with books, could most easily
open by their knocking the door of our heart, and
find a fit resting-place in our affection and favour.
In so much did we receive those who brought books,
that the multitude of those who had preceded them
did not lessen the welcome of the after-comers, nor

were the favours we had awarded yesterday preju-
dicial to those of to-day.   Wherefore, ever using all
the persons we have named as a kind of magnets to
attract books, we had the desired accession of the
vessels of science and a multitudinous flight of the
finest volumes.

And this is what we undertook to narrate in the
present chapter.

CHAPTER IX

HOW, ALTHOUGH WE PREFERRED THE WORKS OF THE ANCIENTS, WE HAVE NOT CONDEMNED THE STUDIES OF THE MODERNS

ALTHOUGH the novelties of the moderns were never disagreeable to our desires, who have always cherished with grateful affection those who devote themselves to study and who add anything either ingenious or useful to the opinions of our forefathers, yet we have always desired with more undoubting avidity to investigate the well-tested labours of the ancients. For whether they had by nature a greater vigour of mental sagacity, or whether they perhaps indulged in closer application to study, or whether they were assisted in their progress by both these things, one thing we are perfectly clear about, that their successors are barely capable of discussing the discoveries of their forerunners, and of acquiring those things as 'pupils which the ancients dug out by difficult efforts of discovery. For as we read that the men of old were of a more excellent degree of bodily development than modern times are found to produce, it is by no means absurd to suppose that most of the ancients were distinguished by brighter faculties, seeing that in the labours they accomplished of both kinds they are inimitable by posterity. And so Phocas writes in the prologue to his Grammar :

> Since all things have been said by men of sense,
> The only novelty is—to condense.

But in truth, if we speak of fervour of learning and diligence in study, they gave up all their lives to philosophy ; while nowadays our contemporaries carelessly spend a few years of hot youth, alternating with the excesses of vice, and when the passions have been calmed, and they have attained the capacity of discerning truth so difficult to discover, they soon become involved in worldly affairs and retire, bidding farewell to the schools of philosophy. They offer the fuming must of their youthful intellect to the difficulties of philosophy, and bestow the clearer wine upon the money-making business of life. Further, as Ovid in the first book of the *De Vetula* justly complains :

> The hearts of all men after gold aspire ;
> Few study to be wise, more to acquire :
> Thus, Science ! all thy virgin charms are sold,
> Whose chaste embraces should disdain their gold,
> Who seek not thee thyself, but pelf through thee,
> Longing for riches, not philosophy.

And further on :

> Thus Philosophy is seen
> Exiled, and Philopecuny is queen,

which is known to be the most violent poison of learning.

How the ancients indeed regarded life as the only limit of study, is shown by Valerius, in his book addressed to Tiberius, by many examples. Carneades, he says, was a laborious and lifelong soldier of wisdom : after he had lived ninety years, the same day put an end to his life and his philosophizing. Isocrates in his ninety-fourth year wrote a most noble work. Sophocles did the same when nearly a hundred years old. Simonides wrote poems in his eightieth year. Aulus Gellius did not desire to live longer than he

should be able to write, as he says himself in the prologue to the *Noctes Atticæ*.

The fervour of study which possessed Euclid the
Socratic, Taurus the philosopher used to relate to
incite young men to study, as Gellius tells in the
book we have mentioned. For the Athenians, hating
the people of Megara, decreed that if any of the
Megarensians entered Athens, he should be put to
death. Then Euclid, who was a Megarensian, and
had attended the lectures of Socrates before this
decree, disguising himself in a woman's dress, used to
go from Megara to Athens by night to hear Socrates,
a distance of twenty miles and back. Imprudent
and excessive was the fervour of Archimedes, a lover
of geometry, who would not declare his name, nor
lift his head from the diagram he had drawn, by
which he might have prolonged his life, but thinking
more of study than of life dyed with his life-blood
the figure he was studying.

There are very many such examples of our pro-
position, but the brevity we aim at does not allow us
to recall them. But, painful to relate, the clerks who
are famous in these days pursue a very different
course. Afflicted with ambition in their tender
years, and slightly fastening to their untried arms the

Icarian wings of presumption, they prematurely snatch the master's cap ; and mere boys become unworthy professors of the several faculties, through which they do not make their way step by step, but like goats ascend by leaps and bounds ; and, having slightly tasted of the mighty stream, they think that they have drunk it dry, though their throats are hardly moistened.   And because they are not grounded in the first rudiments at the fitting time, they build a tottering edifice on an unstable foundation, and now that they have grown up, they are ashamed to learn what they ought to have learned while young, and thus they are compelled to suffer for ever for too hastily jumping at dignities they have not deserved.   For these and the like reasons the tyros in the schools do not attain to the solid learning of the ancients in a few short hours of study, although they may enjoy distinctions, may be accorded titles, be authorized by official robes, and solemnly installed in the chairs of the elders.   Just snatched from the cradle and hastily weaned, they mouth the rules of Priscian and Donatus ; while still beardless boys they gabble with childish stammering the Categories and *Peri Hermeneias*, in the writing of which the great Aristotle is said to have dipped his pen in his heart's blood.   Passing

through these faculties with baneful haste and a harmful diploma, they lay violent hands upon Moses, and
sprinkling about their faces dark waters and thick
clouds of the skies, they offer their heads, unhonoured
by the snows of age, for the mitre of the pontificate.
This pest is greatly encouraged, and they are helped
to attain this fantastic clericate with such nimble
steps, by Papal provisions obtained by insidious
prayers, and also by the prayers, which may not be
rejected, of cardinals and great men, by the cupidity
of friends and relatives, who, building up Sion in
blood, secure ecclesiastical dignities for their nephews
and pupils, before they are seasoned by the course of
nature or ripeness of learning.

Alas ! by the same disease which we are deploring,
we see that the Palladium of Paris has been carried
off in these sad times of ours, wherein the zeal of
that noble university, whose rays once shed light into
every corner of the world, has grown lukewarm, nay,
is all but frozen. There the pen of every scribe is
now at rest, generations of books no longer succeed
each other, and there is none who begins to take
place as a new author. They wrap up their doctrines
in unskilled discourse, and are losing all propriety of
logic, except that our English subtleties, which they

denounce in public, are the subject of their furtive vigils.

Admirable Minerva seems to bend her course to all the nations of the earth, and reacheth from end to end mightily, that she may reveal herself to all mankind. We see that she has already visited the Indians, the Babylonians, the Egyptians and Greeks, the Arabs and the Romans. Now she has passed by Paris, and now has happily come to Britain, the most noble of islands, nay, rather a microcosm in itself, that she may show herself a debtor both to the Greeks and to the Barbarians. At which wondrous sight it is conceived by most men, that as philosophy is now lukewarm in France, so her soldiery are unmanned and languishing.

CHAPTER X

OF THE GRADUAL PERFECTING OF BOOKS

WHILE assiduously seeking out the wisdom of the men of old, according to the counsel of the Wise Man (Eccles. xxxix.) : The wise man, he says, will seek out the wisdom of all the ancients, we have not thought fit to be misled into the opinion that the first founders of the arts have purged away all crudeness, knowing that the discoveries of each of the faithful, when weighed in a faithful balance, makes a tiny portion of science, but that by the anxious investigations of a multitude of scholars, each as it were contributing his share, the mighty bodies of the sciences have grown by successive augmentations to the immense bulk that we now behold. For the disciples, continally melting down the doctrines of their masters, and passing them again

72

through the furnace, drove off the dross that had been previously overlooked, until there came out refined gold tried in a furnace of earth, purified seven times to perfection, and stained by no admixture of error or doubt.

For not even Aristotle, although a man of gigantic intellect, in whom it pleased Nature to try how much of reason she could bestow upon mortality, and whom the Most High made only a little lower than the angels, sucked from his own fingers those wonderful volumes which the whole world can hardly contain. But, on the contrary, with lynx-eyed penetration he had seen through the sacred books of the Hebrews, the Babylonians, the Egyptians, the Chaldæans, the Persians and the Medes, all of which learned Greece had transferred into her treasuries. Whose true sayings he received, but smoothed away their crudities, pruned their superfluities, supplied their deficiencies, and removed their errors. And he held that we should give thanks not only to those who teach rightly, but even to those who err, as affording the way of more easily investigating truth, as he plainly declares in the second book of his Metaphysics. Thus many learned lawyers contributed to the Pandects, many physicians to the Tegni, and it was by this means

that Avicenna edited his Canon, and Pliny his great
work on Natural History, and Ptolemy the Almagest.

For as in the writers of annals it is not difficult to
see that the later writer always presupposes the earlier,
without whom he could by no means relate the
former times, so too we are to think of the authors of
the sciences. For no man by himself has brought forth
any science, since between the earliest students and
those of the latter time we find intermediaries, ancient
if they be compared with our own age, but modern
if we think of the foundations of learning, and these
men we consider the most learned. What would
Virgil, the chief poet among the Latins, have achieved,
if he had not despoiled Theocritus, Lucretius, and
Homer, and had not ploughed with their heifer?
What, unless again and again he had read somewhat
of Parthenius and Pindar, whose eloquence he could
by no means imitate? What could Sallust, Tully,
Boethius, Macrobius, Lactantius, Martianus, and in
short the whole troop of Latin writers have done, if
they had not seen the productions of Athens or the
volumes of the Greeks? Certes, little would Jerome,
master of three languages, Ambrosius, Augustine,
though he confesses that he hated Greek, or even
Gregory, who is said to have been wholly ignorant of

it, have contributed to the doctrine of the Church, if more learned Greece had not furnished them from its stores. As Rome, watered by the streams of Greece, had earlier brought forth philosophers in the image of the Greeks, in like fashion afterwards it produced doctors of the orthodox faith. The creeds we chant are the sweat of Grecian brows, promulgated by their Councils, and established by the martyrdom of many.

Yet their natural slowness, as it happens, turns to the glory of the Latins, since as they were less learned in their studies, so they were less perverse in their errors. In truth, the Arian heresy had all but eclipsed the whole Church ; the Nestorian wickedness presumed to rave with blasphemous rage against the Virgin, for it would have robbed the Queen of Heaven, not in open fight but in disputation, of her name and character as *Mother of God,* unless the invincible champion Cyril, ready to do single battle, with the help of the Council of Ephesus, had in vehemence of spirit utterly extinguished it. Innumerable are the forms as well as the authors of Greek heresies ; for as they were the original cultivators of our holy faith, so too they were the first sowers of tares, as is shown by veracious history. And thus they went on from bad to worse, because in en-

deavouring to part the seamless vesture of the Lord,
they totally destroyed primitive simplicity of doctrine,
and blinded by the darkness of novelty would fall
into the bottomless pit, unless He provide for them
in His inscrutable prerogative, whose wisdom is past
reckoning.

Let this suffice ; for here we reach the limit of our
power of judgment.   One thing, however, we conclude from the premises, that the ignorance of the
Greek tongue is now a great hindrance to the study
of the Latin writers, since without it the doctrines of
the ancient authors, whether Christian or Gentile,
cannot be understood.   And we must come to a like
judgment as to Arabic in numerous astronomical treatises, and as to Hebrew as regards the text of the Holy
Bible, which deficiencies, indeed, Clement V. provides
for, if only the bishops would faithfully observe what
they so lightly decree.   Wherefore we have taken
care to provide a Greek as well as a Hebrew grammar
for our scholars, with certain other aids, by the help
of which studious readers may greatly inform themselves in the writing, reading, and understanding of
the said tongues, although only the hearing of them
can teach correctness of idiom.

CHAPTER XI

WHY WE HAVE PREFERRED BOOKS OF LIBERAL LEARNING TO BOOKS OF LAW

THAT lucrative practice of positive law, designed for the dispensation of earthly things, the more useful it is found by the children of this world, so much the less does it aid the children of light in comprehending the mysteries of holy writ and the secret sacraments of the faith, seeing that it disposes us peculiarly to the friendship of the world, by which man, as S. James testifies, is made the enemy of God. Law indeed encourages rather than extinguishes the contentions of mankind, which are the result of unbounded greed, by complicated laws, which can be turned either way ; though we know that it was created by jurisconsults and pious princes for the purpose of assuaging these contentions.

But in truth, as the same science deals with contraries, and the power of reason can be used to opposite ends, and at the same the human mind is more inclined to evil, it happens with the practisers of this science that they usually devote themselves to promoting contention rather than peace, and instead of quoting laws according to the intent of the legislator, violently strain the language thereof to effect their own purposes.

Wherefore, although the over-mastering love of books has possessed our mind from boyhood, and to rejoice in their delights has been our only pleasure, yet the appetite for the books of the civil law took less hold of our affections, and we have spent but little labour and expense in acquiring volumes of this kind. For they are useful only as the scorpion in treacle, as Aristotle, the sun of science, has said of logic in his book *De Pomo*. We have noticed a certain manifest difference of nature between law and science, in that every science is delighted and desires to open its inward parts and display the very heart of its principles, and to show forth the roots from which it buds and flourishes, and that the emanation of its springs may be seen of all men ; for thus from the cognate and harmonious light of the truth of con-

clusion to principles, the whole body of science will
be full of light, having no part dark. But laws, on
the contrary, since they are only human enactments
for the regulation of social life, or the yokes of princes
thrown over the necks of their subjects, refuse to be
brought to the standard of synteresis, the origin of
equity, because they feel that they possess more of
arbitrary will than rational judgment. Wherefore
the judgment of the wise for the most part is that
the causes of laws are not a fit subject of discussion.
In truth, many laws acquire force by mere custom,
not by syllogistic necessity, like the arts : as Aristotle,
the Phœbus of the Schools, urges in the second book
of the Politics, where he confutes the policy of
Hippodamus, which holds out rewards to the in-
ventors of new laws, because to abrogate old laws and
establish new ones is to weaken the force of those
which exist. For whatever receives its stability from
use alone must necessarily be brought to nought by
disuse.

From which it is seen clearly enough, that as laws
are neither arts nor sciences, so books of law cannot
properly be called books of art or science. Nor is
this faculty which we may call by a special term
geologia, or the *earthly* science, to be properly num-

bered among the sciences. Now the books of the
liberal arts are so useful to the divine writings, that
without their aid the intellect would vainly aspire to
understand them.

CHAPTER XII

WHY WE HAVE CAUSED BOOKS OF GRAMMAR TO BE SO DILIGENTLY PREPARED

WHILE we were constantly delighting our-selves with the reading of books, which it was our custom to read or have read to us every day, we noticed plainly how much the defective knowledge even of a single word hinders the under-standing, as the meaning of no sentence can be apprehended, if any part of it be not understood. Wherefore we ordered the meanings of foreign words to be noted with particular care, and studied the orthography, prosody, etymology, and syntax in ancient grammarians with unrelaxing carefulness, and took pains to elucidate terms that had grown too obscure by age with suitable explanations, in order to make a smooth path for our students.

This is the whole reason why we took care to replace the antiquated volumes of the grammarians by improved codices, that we might make royal roads, by which our scholars in time to come might attain without stumbling to any science.

CHAPTER XIII

WHY WE HAVE NOT WHOLLY NEGLECTED THE FABLES OF THE POETS

ALL the varieties of attack directed against the poets by the lovers of naked truth may be repelled by a two-fold defence : either that even in an unseemly subject-matter we may learn a charming fashion of speech, or that where a fictitious but becoming subject is handled, natural or historical truth is pursued under the guise of allegorical fiction.

Although it is true that all men naturally desire knowledge, yet they do not all take the same pleasure in learning. On the contrary, when they have experienced the labour of study and find their senses wearied, most men inconsiderately fling away the nut, before they have broken the shell and reached the

kernel.   For man is naturally fond of two things,
namely, freedom from control and some pleasure in
his activity ; for which reason no one without reason
submits himself to the control of others, or willingly
engages in any tedious task.   For pleasure crowns
activity, as beauty is a crown to youth, as Aristotle
truly asserts in the tenth book of the Ethics.   Accordingly the wisdom of the ancients devised a remedy by
which to entice the wanton minds of men by a kind
of pious fraud, the delicate Minerva secretly lurking
beneath the mask of pleasure.   We are wont to allure
children by rewards, that they may cheerfully learn
what we force them to study even though they are
unwilling.   For our fallen nature does not tend to
virtue with the same enthusiasm with which it rushes
into vice.   Horace has expressed this for us in a brief
verse of the *Ars Poetica*, where he says :

All poets sing to profit or delight.

And he has plainly intimated the same thing in
another verse of the same book, where he says :

He hits the mark, who mingles joy with use.

How many students of Euclid have been repelled

by the *Pons Asinorum,* as by a lofty and precipitous
rock, which no help of ladders could enable them to
scale ! *This is a hard saying,* they exclaim, *and who
can receive it.* The child of inconstancy, who ended
by wishing to be transformed into an ass, would perhaps never have given up the study of philosophy, if
he had met him in friendly guise veiled under the
cloak of pleasure ; but anon, astonished by Crato's
chair and struck dumb by his endless questions, as by
a sudden thunderbolt, he saw no refuge but in
flight.

So much we have alleged in defence of the poets ;
and now we proceed to show that those who study
them with proper intent are not to be condemned in
regard to them. For our ignorance of one single
word prevents the understanding of a whole long
sentence, as was assumed in the previous chapter.
As now the sayings of the saints frequently allude to
the inventions of the poets, it must needs happen that
through our not knowing the poem referred to, the
whole meaning of the author is completely obscured,
and assuredly, as Cassiodorus says in his book *Of the
Institutes of Sacred Literature :* Those things are not
to be considered trifles without which great things
cannot come to pass. It follows therefore that

through ignorance of poetry we do not understand Jerome, Augustine, Boethius, Lactantius, Sidonius, and very many others, a catalogue of whom would more than fill a long chapter.

The Venerable Bede has very clearly discussed and determined this doubtful point, as is related by that great compiler Gratian, the repeater of numerous authors, who is as confused in form as he was eager in collecting matter for his compilation. Now he writes in his 37th section: Some read secular literature for pleasure, taking delight in the inventions and elegant language of the poets ; but others study this literature for the sake of scholarship, that by their reading they may learn to detest the errors of the Gentiles and may devoutly apply what they find useful in them to the use of sacred learning. Such men study secular literature in a laudable manner. So far Bede.

Taking this salutary instruction to heart, let the detractors of those who study the poets henceforth hold their peace, and let not those who are ignorant of these things require that others should be as ignorant as themselves, for this is the consolation of the wretched. And therefore let every man see that his own intentions are upright, and he may thus make of any subject, observing the limitations of virtue, a study acceptable to God.   And if he have found profit in poetry, as the great Virgil relates that he had done in Ennius, he will not have done amiss.

CHAPTER XIV

WHO OUGHT TO BE SPECIAL LOVERS OF BOOKS

TO him who recollects what has been said before, it is plain and evident who ought to be the chief lovers of books. For those who have most need of wisdom in order to perform usefully the duties of their position, they are without doubt most especially bound to show more abundantly to the sacred vessels of wisdom the anxious affection of a grateful heart. Now it is the office of the wise man to order rightly both himself and others, according to the Phœbus of philosophers, Aristotle, who deceives not nor is deceived in human things. Wherefore princes and prelates, judges and doctors, and all other leaders of the commonwealth, as more than others they have need of wisdom, so more than others ought they to show zeal for the vessels of wisdom.

Boethius, indeed, beheld Philosophy bearing a

sceptre in her left hand and books in her right, by which it is evidently shown to all men that no one can rightly rule a commonwealth without books. Thou, says Boethius, speaking to Philosophy, hast sanctioned this saying by the mouth of Plato, that states would be happy if they were ruled by students of philosophy, or if their rulers would study philosophy. And again, we are taught by the very gesture of the figure that in so far as the right hand is better than the left, so far the contemplative life is more worthy than the active life ; and at the same time we are shown that the business of the wise man is to devote himself by turns, now to the study of truth, and now to the dispensation of temporal things.

We read that Philip thanked the Gods devoutly for having granted that Alexander should be born in the time of Aristotle, so that educated under his instruction he might be worthy to rule his father's empire. While Phaeton unskilled in driving becomes the charioteer of his father's car, he unhappily distributes to mankind the heat of Phœbus, now by excessive nearness, and now by withdrawing it too far, and so, lest all beneath him should be imperilled by the closeness of his driving, justly deserved to be struck by the thunderbolt.

The history of the Greeks as well as Romans shows that there were no famous princes among them who were devoid of literature. The sacred law of Moses in prescribing to the king a rule of government, enjoins him to have a copy made of the book of Divine law (Deut. xvii.) according to the copy shown by the priests, in which he was to read all the days of his life. Certes, God Himself, who hath made and who fashioneth every day the hearts of every one of us, knows the feebleness of human memory and the instability of virtuous intentions in mankind. Wherefore He has willed that books should be as it were an antidote to all evil, the reading and use of which He has commanded to be the healthful daily nourishment of the soul, so that by them the intellect being refreshed and neither weak nor doubtful should never hesitate in action. This subject is elegantly handled by John of Salisbury, in his *Policraticon*. In conclusion, all classes of men who are conspicuous by the tonsure or the sign of clerkship, against whom books lifted up their voices in the fourth, fifth, and sixth chapters, are bound to serve books with perpetual veneration.

CHAPTER XV

OF THE ADVANTAGES OF THE LOVE OF BOOKS

IT transcends the power of human intellect, however deeply it may have drunk of the Pegasean fount, to develop fully the title of the present chapter. Though one should speak with the tongue of men and angels, though he should become a Mercury or Tully, though he should grow sweet with the milky eloquence of Livy, yet he will plead the stammering of Moses, or with Jeremiah will confess that he is but a boy and cannot speak, or will imitate Echo rebounding from the mountains. For we know that the love of books is the same thing as the love of wisdom, as was proved in the second chapter. Now this love is called by the Greek word *philosophy*, the whole virtue of which no created intelligence can comprehend; for she is believed to be the mother of all good things : Wisdom vii. She as a heavenly dew extinguishes the heats of fleshly vices, the intense activity of the mental forces relaxing the vigour of the animal forces, and slothfulness being wholly put to flight, which being gone all the bows of Cupid are unstrung.

Hence Plato says in the *Phædo:* The philosopher is manifest in this, that he dissevers the soul from communion with the body. Love, says Jerome, the knowledge of the scriptures, and thou wilt not love the vices of the flesh. The godlike Xenocrates showed this by the firmness of his reason, who was declared by the famous hetæra Phryne to be a statue and not a man, when all her blandishments could not shake his resolve, as Valerius Maximus relates at length. Our own Origen showed this also, who chose rather to be unsexed by the mutilation of himself, than to be made effeminate by the omnipotence of woman—though it was a hasty remedy, repugnant alike to nature and to virtue, whose place it is not to make men insensible to passion, but to slay with the dagger of reason the passions that spring from instinct.

Again, all who are smitten with the love of books think cheaply of the world and wealth ; as Jerome

says to Vigilantius : The same man cannot love both
gold and books. And thus it has been said in
verse :

> No iron-stained hand is fit to handle books,
> Nor he whose heart on gold so gladly looks :
> The same men love not books and money both,
> And books thy herd, O Epicurus, loathe ;
> Misers and bookmen make poor company,
> Nor dwell in peace beneath the same roof-tree.

No man, therefore, can serve both books and Mammon.

The hideousness of vice is greatly reprobated in
books, so that he who loves to commune with books
is led to detest all manner of vice. The demon, who
derives his name from knowledge, is most effectually
defeated by the knowledge of books, and through
books his multitudinous deceits and the endless labyrinths of his guile are laid bare to those who read,
lest he be transformed into an angel of light and cir-
cumvent the innocent by his wiles. The reverence
of God is revealed to us by books, the virtues by
which He is worshipped are more expressly mani-
fested, and the rewards are described that are
promised by the truth, which deceives not, neither
is deceived. The truest likeness of the beatitude to
come is the contemplation of the sacred writings, in

which we behold in turn the Creator and the creature, and draw from streams of perpetual gladness. Faith is established by the power of books ; hope is strengthened by their solace, insomuch that by patience and the consolation of scripture we are in good hope. Charity is not puffed up, but is edified by the knowledge of true learning, and, indeed, it is clearer than light that the Church is established upon the sacred writings.

Books delight us, when prosperity smiles upon us ; they comfort us inseparably when stormy fortune frowns on us. They lend validity to human compacts, and no serious judgments are propounded without their help. Arts and sciences, all the advantages of which no mind can enumerate, consist in books. How highly must we estimate the wondrous power of books, since through them we survey the utmost bounds of the world and time, and contemplate the things that are as well as those that are not, as it were in the mirror of eternity. In books we climb mountains and scan the deepest gulfs of the abyss ; in books we behold the finny tribes that may not exist outside their native waters, distinguish the properties of streams and springs and of various lands ; from books we dig out gems and metals and the materials of every kind of mineral, and learn the virtues of herbs and trees and plants, and survey at will the whole progeny of Neptune, Ceres, and Pluto.

But if we please to visit the heavenly inhabitants, Taurus, Caucasus, and Olympus are at hand, from which we pass beyond the realms of Juno and mark out the territories of the seven planets by lines and circles. And finally we traverse the loftiest firmament of all, adorned with signs, degrees, and figures in the utmost variety. There we inspect the antarctic pole, which eye hath not seen, nor ear heard ; we admire the luminous Milky Way and the Zodiac, marvellously and delightfully pictured with celestial animals. Thence by books we pass on to separate substances, that the intellect may greet kindred intelligences, and with the mind's eye may discern the First Cause of all things and the Unmoved Mover of infinite virtue, and may immerse itself in love without end. See how with the aid of books we attain the reward of our beatitude, while we are yet sojourners below.

Why need we say more ? Certes, just as we have learnt on the authority of Seneca, leisure without letters is death and the sepulture of the living, so contrariwise we conclude that occupation with letters or books is the life of man.

Again, by means of books we communicate to friends as well as foes what we cannot safely entrust to messengers ; since the book is generally allowed access to the chambers of princes, from which the voice of its author would be rigidly excluded, as Tertullian observes at the beginning of his *Apologeticus*. When shut up in prison and in bonds, and utterly deprived of bodily liberty, we use books as ambassadors to our friends, and entrust them with the conduct of our cause, and send them where to go ourselves would incur the penalty of death. By the aid of books we remember things that are past, and even prophesy as to the future ; and things present, which shift and flow, we perpetuate by committing them to writing.

The felicitous studiousness and the studious felicity of the all-powerful eunuch, of whom we are told in the Acts, who had been so mightily kindled by the love of the prophetic writings that he ceased not from his reading by reason of his journey, had banished all thought of the populous palace of Queen Candace, and had forgotten even the treasures of which he was the keeper, and had neglected alike his journey and the chariot in which he rode. Love of his book alone had wholly engrossed this domicile of chastity, under whose guidance he soon deserved to enter the gate of faith. O gracious love of books, which by the grace of baptism transformed the child of Gehenna and nursling of Tartarus into a Son of the Kingdom !

Let the feeble pen now cease from the tenor of an infinite task, lest it seem foolishly to undertake what in the beginning it confessed to be impossible to any.

CHAPTER XVI

THAT IT IS MERITORIOUS TO WRITE NEW
BOOKS AND TO RENEW THE OLD

JUST as it is necessary for the state to prepare arms and to provide abundant stores of victuals for the soldiers who are to fight for it, so it is fitting for the Church Militant to fortify itself against the assaults of pagans and heretics with a multitude of sound writings.

But because all the appliances of mortal men with the lapse of time suffer the decay of mortality, it is needful to replace the volumes that are worn out with age by fresh successors, that the perpetuity of which the individual is by its nature incapable may be secured to the species ; and hence it is that the Preacher says : *Of making many books there is no end.* For as the bodies of books, seeing that they are

formed of a combination of contrary elements, undergo a continual dissolution of their structure, so by
the forethought of the clergy a remedy should be
found, by means of which the sacred book paying the
debt of nature may obtain a natural heir and may
raise up like seed to its dead brother, and thus may
be verified that saying of Ecclesiasticus : His father
is dead, and he is as if he were not dead ; for he
hath left one behind him that is like himself.   And
thus the transcription of ancient books is as it were
the begetting of fresh sons, on whom the office of
the father may devolve, lest it suffer detriment. Now
such transcribers are called *antiquarii*, whose occupations Cassiodorus confesses please him above all the
tasks of bodily labour, adding : " Happy effort," he
says, " laudable industry, to preach to men with the
hand, to let loose tongues with the fingers, silently to
give salvation to mortals, and to fight with pen and
ink against the illicit wiles of the Evil One."   So far
Cassiodorus.   Moreover, our Saviour exercised the
office of the scribe when He stooped down and with
His finger wrote on the ground (John viii.), that
no one, however exalted, may think it unworthy of
him to do what he sees the wisdom of God the
Father did.

O singular serenity of writing, to practise which the Artificer of the world stoops down, at whose dread name every knee doth bow !   O venerable handicraft pre-eminent above all other crafts that are practised by the hand of man, to which our Lord humbly inclines His breast, to which the finger of God is applied, performing the office of a pen !   We do not read of the Son of God that He sowed or ploughed, wove or digged ; nor did any other of the mechanic arts befit the divine wisdom incarnate except to trace letters in writing, that every gentleman and sciolist may know that fingers are given by God to men for the task of writing rather than for war.   Wherefore we entirely approve the judgment of books, wherein they declared in our sixth chapter the clerk who can not write to be as it were disabled.

God himself inscribes the just in the book of the living ; Moses received the tables of stone written with the finger of God.   Job desires that he himself that judgeth would write a book.   Belshazzar trembled when he saw the fingers of a man's hand writing upon the wall, *Mene tekel phares*.   I wrote, says Jeremiah, with ink in the book.   Christ bids his beloved disciple John, What thou seest write in a book.   So the office of the writer is enjoined on Isaiah and on Joshua, that

the act and skill of writing may be commended to
future generations. Christ Himself has written on His
vesture and on His thigh *King of Kings and Lord of
Lords*, so that without writing the royal ornaments of
the Omnipotent cannot be made perfect. Being
dead they cease not to teach, who write books of sacred
learning. Paul did more for building up the fabric of
the Church by writing his holy epistles, than by
preaching by word of mouth to Jews and Gentiles.
He who has attained the prize continues daily by
books, what he long ago began while a sojourner
upon the earth ; and thus is fulfilled in the doctors
writing books the saying of the Prophet : They that
turn many to righteousness shall be as the stars for
ever and ever.

Moreover, it has been determined by the doctors of
the Church that the longevity of the ancients, before
God destroyed the original world by the Deluge, is to
be ascribed to a miracle and not to nature ; as though
God granted to them such length of days as was required for finding out the sciences and writing them
in books ; amongst which the wonderful variety of
astronomy required, according to Josephus, a period of
six hundred years, to submit it to ocular observation.
Nor, indeed, do they deny that the fruits of the earth

in that primitive age afforded a more nutritious ali-
ment to men than in our modern times, and thus they
had not only a livelier energy of body, but also a more
lengthened period of vigour ; to which it contributed
not a little that they lived according to virtue and
denied themselves all luxurious delights.   Whoever
therefore is by the good gift of God endowed with
gift of science, let him, according to the counsel of the
Holy Spirit, write wisdom in his time of leisure
(Ecclus. xxxviii.), that his reward may be with the blessed
and his days may be lengthened in this present world.

And further, if we turn our discourse to the princes
of the world, we find that famous emperors not only
attained excellent skill in the art of writing, but indulged greatly in its practice.   Julius Cæsar, the first
and greatest of them all, has left us Commentaries on
the Gallic and the Civil Wars written by himself ; he
wrote also two books *De Analogia*, and two books of
Anticatones, and a poem called *Iter*, and many other
works.   Julius and Augustus devised means of writing
one letter for another, and so concealing what they
wrote.   For Julius put the fourth letter for the first, and
so on through the alphabet ; whilst Augustus used the
second for the first, the third for the second, and so
throughout.   He is said in the greatest difficulties of

affairs during the Mutinensian War to have read and
written and even declaimed every day. Tiberius wrote
a lyric poem and some Greek verses. Claudius likewise
was skilled in both Greek and Latin, and wrote several
books. But Titus was skilled above all men in the
art of writing, and easily imitated any hand he chose;
so that he used to say that if he had wished it he might
have become a most skilful forger. All these things
are noted by Suetonius in his Lives of the XII. Cæsars.

CHAPTER XVII

OF SHOWING DUE PROPRIETY IN THE CUSTODY
OF BOOKS

WE are not only rendering service to God in
preparing volumes of new books, but also
exercising an office of sacred piety when we treat
books carefully, and again when we restore them to
their proper places and commend them to inviolable
custody ; that they may rejoice in purity while we
have them in our hands, and rest securely when
they are put back in their repositories. And surely
next to the vestments and vessels dedicated to the
Lord's body, holy books deserve to be rightly treated
by the clergy, to which great injury is done so often
as they are touched by unclean hands. Wherefore
we deem it expedient to warn our students of various
negligences, which might always be easily avoided
and do wonderful harm to books.

And in the first place as to the opening and closing of books, let there be due moderation, that they be not unclasped in precipitate haste, nor when we have finished our inspection be put away without being duly closed. For it behoves us to guard a book much more carefully than a boot.

But the race of scholars is commonly badly brought up, and unless they are bridled in by the rules of their elders they indulge in infinite puerilities. They behave with petulance, and are puffed up with presumption, judging of everything as if they were certain, though they are altogether inexperienced.

You may happen to see some headstrong youth lazily lounging over his studies, and when the winter's frost is sharp, his nose running from the nipping cold drips down, nor does he think of wiping it with his pocket-handkerchief until he has bedewed the book before him with the ugly moisture. Would that he had before him no book, but a cobbler's apron ! His nails are stuffed with fetid filth as black as jet, with which he marks any passage that pleases him. He distributes a multitude of straws, which he inserts to stick out in different places, so that the halm may remind him of what his memory cannot retain. These straws, because the book has no stomach to digest them, and no one takes them out, first distend the book from its wonted closing, and at length, being carelessly abandoned to oblivion, go to decay. He does not fear to eat fruit or cheese over an open book, or carelessly to carry a cup to and from his mouth ; and because he has no wallet at hand he drops into books the fragments that are left. Continually chattering, he is never weary of disputing with his companions, and while he alleges a crowd of senseless arguments, he wets the book lying half open in his lap with sputtering showers. Aye, and then hastily folding his arms he leans forward on the book, and by a brief spell of study invites a prolonged nap ; and then, by way of mending the wrinkles, he folds back the margin of the leaves, to the no small injury of the book. Now the rain is over and gone, and the flowers have appeared in our land. Then the scholar we are speaking of, a neglecter rather than an inspecter of books, will stuff his volume with violets, and primroses, with roses and quatrefoil. Then he will use his wet and perspiring hands to turn over the volumes ; then he will thump the white vellum with gloves covered with all kinds of dust, and with his finger clad in long-used leather will hunt line by line through the page ; then at the sting of the biting flea the sacred book is flung

aside, and is hardly shut for another month, until it is
so full of the dust that has found its way within, that
it resists the effort to close it.

But the handling of books is specially to be forbidden to those shameless youths, who as soon as they
have learned to form the shapes of letters, straightway,
if they have the opportunity, become unhappy com-
mentators, and wherever they find an extra margin
about the text, furnish it with monstrous alphabets,
or if any other frivolity strikes their fancy, at once
their pen begins to write it. There the Latinist and
sophister and every unlearned writer tries the fitness
of his pen, a practice that we have frequently seen
injuring the usefulness and value of the most beautiful
books.

Again, there is a class of thieves shamefully mutilat-
ing books, who cut away the margins from the sides
to use as material for letters, leaving only the text, or
employ the leaves from the ends, inserted for the
protection of the book, for various uses and abuses—
a kind of sacrilege which should be prohibited by the
threat of anathema.

Again, it is part of the decency of scholars that
whenever they return from meals to their study,
washing should invariably precede reading, and that

no grease-stained finger should unfasten the clasps, or turn the leaves of a book. Nor let a crying child admire the pictures in the capital letters, lest he soil the parchment with wet fingers ; for a child instantly touches whatever he sees. Moreover, the laity, who look at a book turned upside down just as if it were open in the right way, are utterly unworthy of any communion with books. Let the clerk take care also that the smutty scullion reeking from his stewpots does not touch the lily leaves of books, all unwashed, but he who walketh without blemish shall minister to the precious volumes. And, again, the cleanliness of decent hands would be of great benefit to books as well as scholars, if it were not that the itch and pimples are characteristic of the clergy.

Whenever defects are noticed in books, they should be promptly repaired, since nothing spreads more quickly than a tear and a rent which is neglected at the time will have to be repaired afterwards with usury.

Moses, the gentlest of men, teaches us to make bookcases most neatly, wherein they may be protected from any injury : *Take*, he says, *this book of the law, and put it in the side of the ark of the covenant of the Lord your God.* O fitting place and appropriate for a library, which was made of imperishable shittim-wood, and was all covered within and without with gold ! But the Saviour also has warned us by His example against all unbecoming carelessness in the handling of books, as we read in S. Luke.   For when He had read the scriptural prophecy of Himself in the book that was delivered to Him, He did not give it again to the minister, until He had closed it with his own most sacred hands.   By which students are most clearly taught that in the care of books the merest trifles ought not to be neglected.

CHAPTER XVIII

SHOWETH THAT WE HAVE COLLECTED SO GREAT STORE OF BOOKS FOR THE COMMON BENEFIT OF SCHOLARS AND NOT ONLY FOR OUR OWN PLEASURE

NOTHING in human affairs is more unjust than that those things which are most righteously done, should be perverted by the slanders of malicious men, and that one should bear the reproach of sin where he has rather deserved the hope of honour. Many things are done with singleness of eye, the right hand knoweth not what the left hand doth, the lump is uncorrupted by leaven, nor is the garment woven of wool and linen ; and yet by the trickery of perverse men a pious work is mendaciously transformed into some monstrous act. Certes, such is the unhappy condition of sinful nature, that not merely in acts that are morally doubtful it adopts the worse conclusion ; but often it depraves by iniquitous subversion those which have the appearance of rectitude.

For although the love of books from the nature of its object bears the aspect of goodness, yet, wonderful to say, it has rendered us obnoxious to the censures of many, by whose astonishment we were disparaged and censured, now for excess of curiosity, now for the exhibition of vanity, now for intemperance of delight in literature ; though indeed we were no more disturbed by their vituperation than by the barking of so many dogs, satisfied with the testimony of Him to whom it appertaineth to try the hearts and reins. For as the aim and purpose of our inmost will is inscrutable to men and is seen of God alone, the searcher of hearts, they deserve to be rebuked for their pernicious temerity, who so eagerly set a mark of condemnation upon human acts, the ultimate springs of which they cannot see. For the final end in matters of conduct holds the same position as first principles in speculative science or axioms in mathematics, as the chief of philosophers, Aristotle, points out in the seventh book of the Ethics. And therefore, just as the truth of our conclusions depends upon the correctness of our premises, so in matters of action the stamp of moral rectitude is given by the honesty of aim and purpose, in cases where the act itself would otherwise be held to be morally indifferent.

Now we have long cherished in our heart of hearts the fixed resolve, when Providence should grant a favourable opportunity, to found in perpetual charity a Hall in the reverend university of Oxford, the chief nursing mother of all liberal arts, and to endow it with the necessary revenues, for the maintenance of a number of scholars; and moreover to enrich the Hall with the treasures of our books, that all and every of them should be in common as regards their use and study, not only to the scholars of the said Hall, but by their means to all the students of the before-named university for ever, in the form and manner which the following chapter shall declare. Wherefore the sincere love of study and zeal for the strengthening of the orthodox faith to the edifying of the Church, have begotten in us that solicitude so marvellous to the lovers of pelf, of collecting books wherever they were to be purchased, regardless of expense, and of having those that could not he bought fairly transcribed.

For as the favourite occupations of men are variously distinguished according to the disposition of the heavenly bodies, which frequently control our natural composition, so that some men choose to devote themselves to architecture, others to agriculture, others to hunting, others to navigation, others to war, others to games, we have under the aspect of Mercury entertained a blameless pleasure in books, which under the rule of right reason, over which no stars are dominant, we have ordered to the glory of the Supreme Being, that where our minds found tranquillity and peace, thence also might spring a most devout service of God. And therefore let our detractors cease, who are as blind men judging of colours ; let not bats venture to speak of light ; and let not those who carry beams in their own eyes presume to pull the mote out of their brother's eye. Let them cease to jeer with satirical taunts at things of which they are ignorant, and to discuss hidden things that are not revealed to the eyes of men ; who perchance would have praised and commended us, if we had spent our time in hunting, dice-playing, or courting the smiles of ladies.

CHAPTER XIX

OF THE MANNER OF LENDING ALL OUR BOOKS TO STUDENTS

IT has ever been difficult so to restrain men by the laws of rectitude, that the astuteness of successors might not strive to transgress the bounds of their predecessors, and to infringe established rules in insolence of licence. Accordingly, with the advice of prudent men, we have prescribed the manner in which we desire that the communication and use of our books should be permitted for the benefit of students.

Imprimis, we give and grant all and singular the books, of which we have made a special catalogue, in consideration of affection, to the community of scholars living in ———— Hall at Oxford, as a perpetual gift, for our soul and the souls of our parents, and also for the soul of the most illustrious King

Edward the Third from the Conquest, and of the most pious Queen Philippa, his consort : to the intent that the same books may be lent from time to time to all and singular the scholars and masters of the said place, as well regular as secular, for the advancement and use of study, in the manner immediately following, that is to say :

Five of the scholars sojourning in the Hall aforesaid shall be appointed by the Master thereof, who shall have the charge of all the books, of which five persons three and not fewer may lend any book or books for inspection and study ; but for copying or transcribing we direct that no book shall be allowed outside the walls of the house. Therefore, when any scholar secular or religious, whom for this purpose we regard with equal favour, shall seek to borrow any book, let the keepers diligently consider if they have a duplicate of the said book, and if so, let them lend him the book, taking such pledge as in their judgment exceeds the value of the book delivered, and let a record be made forthwith of the pledge and of the book lent, containing the names of the persons delivering the book and of the person who receives it, together with the day and year when the loan is made.

But if the keepers find that the book asked for is not in duplicate, they shall not lend such book to any one whomsoever, unless he shall belong to the community of scholars of the said Hall, unless perhaps for inspection within the walls of the aforesaid house or Hall, but not to be carried beyond it.

But to any of the scholars of the said Hall, any book may be lent by three of the aforesaid keepers, after first recording, however, his name, with the day on which he receives the book. Nevertheless, the borrower may not lend the book entrusted to him to another, except with the permission of three of the aforesaid keepers, and then the name of the first borrower being erased, the name of the second with the time of delivery is to be recorded.

Each keeper shall take an oath to observe all these regulations when they enter upon the charge of the books. And the recipients of any book or books shall thereupon swear that they will not use the book or books for any other purpose but that of inspection or study, and that they will not take or permit to be taken it or them beyond the town and suburbs of Oxford.

Moreover, every year the aforesaid keepers shall render an account to the Master of the House and two of his scholars whom he shall associate with himself, or if he shall not be at leisure, he shall appoint three inspectors, other than the keepers, who shall peruse the catalogue of books, and see that they have them all, either in the volumes themselves or at least as represented by deposits. And the more fitting season for rendering this account we believe to be from the First of July until the festival of the Translation of the Glorious Martyr S. Thomas next following.

We add this further provision, that anyone to whom a book has been lent, shall once a year exhibit it to the keepers, and shall, if he wishes it, see his pledge. Moreover, if it chances that a book is lost by death, theft, fraud, or carelessness, he who has lost it or his representative or executor shall pay the value of the book and receive back his deposit. But if in any wise any profit shall accrue to the keepers, it shall not be applied to any purpose but the repair and maintenance of the books.

CHAPTER XX

AN EXHORTATION TO SCHOLARS TO REQUITE US
BY PIOUS PRAYERS

TIME now clamours for us to terminate this
treatise which we have composed concerning
the love of books ; in which we have endeavoured
to give the astonishment of our contemporaries the
reason why we have loved books so greatly.   But
because it is hardly granted to mortals to accomplish
aught that is not rolled in the dust of vanity, we
do not venture entirely to justify the zealous love
which we have so long had for books, or to deny
that it may perchance sometimes have been the
occasion of some venial negligence, albeit the object
of our love is honourable and our intention upright.
For if when we have done everything, we are
bound to call ourselves unprofitable servants ; if
the most holy Job was afraid of all his works ; if

according to Isaiah all our righteousness is as filthy
rags, who shall presume to boast himself of the perfection of any virtue, or deny that from some circum-
stance a thing may deserve to be reprehended, which
in itself perhaps was not reprehensible. For good
springs from one selfsame source, but evil arises in
many ways, as Dionysius informs us. Wherefore to
make amends for our iniquities, by which we acknow-
ledge ourselves to have frequently offended the Creator of all things, in asking the assistance of their
prayers, we have thought fit to exhort our future
students to show their gratitude as well to us as to
their other benefactors in time to come by requiting
our forethought for their benefit by spiritual retribu-
tion. Let us live when dead in their memories, who
have lived in our benevolence before they were born,
and live now sustained by our beneficence. Let
them implore the mercy of the Redeemer with unwearied prayer, that the pious Judge may excuse our
negligences, may pardon the wickedness of our sins,
may cover the lapses of our feebleness with the cloak
of piety, and remit by His divine goodness the
offences of which we are ashamed and penitent.
That He may preserve to us for a due season of
repentance the gifts of His good grace, steadfastness

of faith, loftiness of hope, and the widest charity to all men. That He may turn our haughty will to lament its faults, that it may deplore its past most vain elations, may retract its most bitter indignations, and detest its most insane delectations. That His virtue may abound in us, when our own is found wanting, and that He who freely consecrated our beginning by the sacrament of baptism, and advanced our progress to the seat of the Apostles without any desert of ours, may deign to fortify our outgoing by the fitting sacraments. That we may be delivered from the lust of the flesh, that the fear of death may utterly vanish and our spirit may desire to be dissolved and be with Christ, and existing upon earth in body only, in thought and longing our conversation may be in Heaven. That the Father of mercies and the God of all consolation may graciously come to meet the prodigal returning from the husks ; that He may receive the piece of silver that has been lately found and transmit it by His holy angels into His eternal treasury. That He may rebuke with His terrible countenance, at the hour of our departure, the spirits of darkness, lest Leviathan, that old serpent, lying hid at the gate of death, should spread unforeseen snares for our feet. But when we shall be summoned to

the awful judgment-seat to give an account on the
testimony of conscience of all things we have done in
the body, the God-Man may consider the price of
the holy blood that He has shed, and that the Incarnate Deity may note the frame of our carnal nature,
that our weakness may pass unpunished where infinite
loving-kindness is to be found, and that the soul of
the wretched sinner may breathe again where the
peculiar office of the Judge is to show mercy.   And
further, let our students be always diligent in invoking
the refuge of our hope after God, the Virgin Mother
of God and Blessed Queen of Heaven, that we who
for our manifold sins and wickednesses have deserved
the anger of the Judge, by the aid of her ever-accept-
able supplications may merit His forgiveness ; that
her pious hand may depress the scale of the balance
in which our small and few good deeds shall be
weighed, lest the heaviness of our sins preponderate
and cast us down to the bottomless pit of perdition.
Moreover, let them ever venerate with due observance
the most deserving Confessor Cuthbert, the care of
whose flock we have unworthily undertaken, ever devoutly praying that he may deign to excuse by his
prayers his all-unworthy vicar, and may procure him
whom he hath admitted as his successor upon earth to

be made his assessor in Heaven.   Finally, let them pray God with holy prayers as well of body as of soul, that He will restore the spirit created in the image of the Trinity, after its sojourn in this miserable world, to its primordial prototype, and grant to it for ever to enjoy the sight of His countenance : through our Lord Jesus Christ.   Amen.

THE END OF THE PHILOBIBLON OF MASTER RICHARD DE
AUNGERVILLE, SURNAMED DE BURY, LATE BISHOP OF
DURHAM.   THIS TREATISE WAS FINISHED IN OUR
MANORHOUSE OF AUCKLAND ON THE 24TH
DAY OF JANUARY, IN THE YEAR OF OUR LORD
ONE   THOUSAND   THREE   HUNDRED   AND
FORTY-FOUR,   THE   FIFTY-EIGHTH
YEAR OF OUR AGE BEING EXACTLY
COMPLETED, AND THE ELEVENTH
YEAR OF OUR PONTIFICATE
DRAWING TO AN END ;
TO   THE   GLORY
OF   GOD.
A M E N.

Notes

PROLOGUE

1, 7. Ps. cxvi. 12.

2, 8. *the Sevenfold Spirit*, "septiformis spiritus," first used by St. Augustine ; *cp.* Isa. xi. 23, and Rev. i. 4.

2, 9. *that it may burn*, Ps. xxxix. 3.

2, 15. *by the atonement of almsgiving, cp.* Dan. iv. 27.

2, 18. *the good will of man, cp.* Phil. i. 15.

3, 1. *a host of unhappy, nay, rather elect scholars,* "grex scholarium elegorum quin potius electorum."

3, 7. *in the cultivated field of youth,* quoted from the anonymous work "*De varietate carminum.*"

3, 9. *bright virtue lurks buried in obscurity.* Boethius, De Consol. Phil. i. m. 5,—"Latet obscuris condita virtus Clara tenebris, justusque tulit Crimen iniqui."

3, 10. *burning lights, cp.* Matt. v. 15.

3, 14. *vines into wild vines, cp.* Isa. v. 2.

3, 15. *olives into the wild olive, cp.* Rom. xi. 24.

3, 21. *the nectared cup of philosophy,* "philosophiæ nectareo poculo," *cp.* the De disciplina Scholarium, C. V.

4, 6. *that little with which Nature is contented, cp.* Boethius, De Cons. Ph. ii. pr. 5.

4, 8. *athletes of the faith, cp.* "athleta Dei," a common phrase for a Christian.

4, 9. *how suddenly the woof is cut*, cp. Job vii. 6; and Isa. xxxviii. 12.

4, 14. *a meteor;* the word used in the original "assub" is derived from the translations of Aristotle made from the Arabic; it is found in Latin-English handbooks of the middle ages glossing "sterre-slyme," *i.e.* the star-jelly, which was supposed to be deposited by falling stars.

I

7, 1. *cp.* Prov. xxi. 20.

7, 2. *which all men desire by an instinct of nature*, cp. Aristotle, Metaphysics, i. i.: πάντες ἄνθρωποι τοῦ εἰδέναι ὀρέγονται φύσει.

7, 3. *infinitely surpasses all the riches of the world*, cp. Wisdom vii. 8. 9.

7, 7. *at whose splendour the sun and the moon are dark to look upon*, cp. Wisdom vii. 29.

7, 9. *are bitter*, cp. Wisdom viii. 16.

7, 10. *that fadeth not*, cp. Wisdom vi. 13.

7, 13. *the Father of lights*, James i. 17.

8, 2. cp. Ecclesiasticus xxiv. 29.

8, 4. *the languishing soul*, cp. Wisdom xvii. 8.

8, 6. *by thee kings reign*, Prov. viii. 15.

8, 13. *into pruning hooks*, "in ligones," cp. Joel iii. 10.

8, 20. *every one who asks*, Matt. vii. 7.

8, 23. *the cherubim*, cp. Exod. xxv. 20.

9, 4. *celestial, terrestrial, and infernal*, Phil. ii. 10.

9, 9. *the chair of Crato;* the name occurs again in Chap. XIII. In both cases the obscure reference is one of difficulty, though the reading is probably correct: in this passage, *Cato* rather than *Crato* would seem better, but the change cannot be warranted, though some MSS. read *Catonis*. *Crato* is mentioned in "the Golden Legend" and elsewhere, as well as in several liturgical hymns.

9, 13. *all things are corrupted*, cp. Aristotle, Phys. iv. 12.

9, 21. *faithful Fabricius and stern Cato, cp.* Boethius, De Cons. Phil. ii. m. 7.

10, 6. *The Almagest;* the Astronomy or Μεγάλη Σύνταξις was probably so called to distinguish it from the Μαθηματική Σύνταξις, or Mathematics of Ptolemy; it was preserved and communicated to Europe by the Arabs, and the name *Almagest* is formed of the Arabic article *al*, and the Greek μεγίστη.

10, 11. *things new and old*, Matt. xiii. 52.

10, 13. *holy to honour before friendship, cp.* Aristotle, Ethics, i. 6. 1.

10, 15. *holy Boethius considers to be threefold, cp.* De Interpret., Migne, lxiv. p. 297.

10, 18. *for the meaning of the voice perishes with the sound, cp.* 1 Cor. xiv. 11.

10, 20. *Wisdom that is hid, cp.* Ecclesiasticus xx. 30.

11, 12. *the vestibule of perception,* "vestibula sensus communis."

12, 4. *given us by the inspiration of God, cp.* 2 Tim. iii. 16.

12, 14. *the golden pots, cp.* Heb. ix. 4.

12, 15. *rocks flowing with honey, cp.* Deut. xxxii. 13.

12, 16. *garners ever full, cp.* Ps. cxliv. 13.

12, 17. *the tree of life, cp.* Gen. ii. 9 ; Rev. xxii. 2.

12, 17. *the fourfold river of Paradise, cp.* Gen. ii. 10.

12, 21. *the troughs, cp.* Gen. xxx. 38.

12, 22. *the stones of testimony, cp.* Josh. iv. 7.

12, 23. *the pitchers holding the lamps, cp.* Judges vii. 16.

13, 1. *the arms of the soldiers, cp.* 2 Cor. x. 4.

13, 3. *darts of the wicked, cp.* Eph. vi. 16.

13, 4. *burning lamps*, Luke xii. 35.

II

15, 17. *the wisest of men ;* no doubt Solomon, *cp.* Ecclus. vii. 15.

15, 17. *the chief of philosophers,* "hierophilosophus," probably Aristotle (*cp.* note above, 10, 13).

15, 19. *Zorobabel, cp.* 1 Esdras iii. 10–12, iv. 13.
18, 1. *cp.* Prov. viii. 11.

III

19, 9. *an infinite treasure, cp.* Wisdom vii. 14.

19, 14. *Solomon the sun of men ;* the phrase occurs in Walter Map's "De Nugis Curialium," iv. 3.

20, 5. *the law of nature, cp.* Renan, Avveroès, p. 55 f. ; the passage referred to is quoted by Roger Bacon, Op. Maj. p. 27, and other mediæval writers.

21, 12. *they are worth all that thou hast, cp.* Gregory xl. Homiliarum in Evangelia, lib. 1. Hom. 5 : "Aestimationem quippe pretii non habet, sed tamen regnum Dei tantum valet, quantum habes."

IV

22, 1. *cp.* Matt. xii. 34.

22, 2. *the ungrateful cuckoo,* from Pliny's Natural History, x. 11.

22, 6. *Bring it again to mind, cp.* Isa. xlvi. 8.

22, 11. *as children, cp.* 1 Cor. xiii. 11.

22, 13. *partakers of our milk, cp.* Heb. v. i3.

23, 4. *the goodly garments, cp.* Gen. xxvii. 15.

23, 7. *as a tablet to be painted on,* "tabula depingenda," *cp.* "tabula rasa."

23, 7. *all the household of philosophy are clothed with garments, cp.* Prov. xxxi. 21.

23, 10. *the fourfold wings of the quadrivials,* the quadrivium included the four sciences—"quatuor pennas"—of music, arithmetic, geometry and astronomy, the trivium included grammar, dialectic, and rhetoric.

23, 12. *we sent you to a friend, cp.* Luke xi. 4–8.

23, 16. *sojourner,* "viator."

23, 21. *ye are a chosen people, cp.* Pet. ii. 9.

23, 22. *a peculiar people, cp.* Deut. vii. 6 ; Exod. xix. 6.

23, 23. *chosen into the lot of God*, "in sortem Domini computati " ; the reference is to the derivation of *clericus*, of or pertaining to an inheritance, Gr. κληρικ-ός, from κλῆρος, a lot or allotment of land.

On the application of κλῆρος to the Christian ministry, see Bp. Lightfoot, *Philippians*, 245–6, where its probable origin is seen in the use of the word in Acts i. 17, " the lot of this ministry." In the time of Jerome explanations were sought in the use of κλῆρος in Deut. xviii. 2, compared with ix. 29 and parallel passages, and 1 Pet. v. 3 was interpreted in this sense. (New English Dict. *sub* Cleric.)

23, 24. *nay, ye are called the very church of God*, " immo vos antonomatice ipsa Ecclesia Dei dicimini," *antonomatici* often wrongly altered to automatici.

24, 2. *serving the altar, cp.* 1 Cor. ix. 13 ; Heb. xiii. 10.

24, 5. *a little higher than the angels, cp.* Heb. ii. 7.

24, 7. *thou art a priest,* Ps. cx. 4.

24, 9. *wherein it is required, cp.* 1 Cor. iv. 2.

24, 19. *are called of men Rabbi, cp.* Matt. xxiii. 7.

24, 21. *great lights, cp.* Phil. ii. 15.

25, 6. *two paths of Phythagoras* ; the letter Y as emblematic of the broad and narrow paths of vice and virtue.

25, 7. *going backwards, cp.* Jer. xv. 6.

25, 13. *by a most shameful death,* Wisdom ii. 20.

25, 14. *your friend is put far away, cp.* Ps. lxxxviii. 18.

25, 15. *Peter swears, cp.* Matt. xxvi. 72.

25, 17. *Crucify, crucify him,* John xix. 6–12.

25, 19. *before the judgment seat, cp.* 2 Cor. v. 10.

25, 22. *the sorrowing Muses,* "Camenæ laceræ," *cp.* Boethius, De Cons. Phil. i. Metr. 1.

26, 5. *the gates of death, cp.* Ps. cvii. 18.

26, 6. *the book he has not forgotten is handed to him to be read* ; this of course refers to the benefit of the clergy—the privilege of exemption from trial by secular court allowed to or claimed by clergymen arraigned for felony ; in later times, the privilege of exemption from sentence which in the case of certain offences might be pleaded on his first conviction by any one who could read : *cp.* the use of *neck verse* ; the ability to read, being originally merely the test of the " clergy," or clerical position, came at length to be in itself the ground of privilege, so that the phrase became=benefit of scholarship. (New English Dict. *sub* Clergy.)

27, 4. *cp.* Ezek. iii. 1–3.

27, 6. *the panther*, *cp.* Pliny's Natural History, viii. 23.

27, 11. " O virtus infinita librorum "; virtus = a host.

28, 10. *that biped beast ;* glossed in sundry old MSS. *scilicet mulier*, which in some editions occurs in the text (*cp.* Blades, " The Enemies of Books ").

28, 13. *the asp and the cocatrice*, *cp.* Ps. xci. 13.

28, 22. *furs ;* MSS. vary between *furraturas, farraturas, folraturas, ferraturas*, and *foderaturas* ; probably merely stuffing or lining of any sort.

28, 25. *Theophrastus ;* the reference is to a book against marriage attributed to Theophrastus by St. Jerome.

28, 25. *Valerius ;* " Valerius ad Rufinum de uxore non ducenda," was one of the most popular of mediæval books ; (*cp.* Chaucer's *Wife of Bath*, Prologue, for the whole of this passage).

29, 7. *our soul is bowed down to the dust*, " adhaesit pavimento anima nostra," from Ps. xliv. 25.

29, 8. *our belly cleaveth unto the earth*, Ps. xliv. 25.

29, 11. *and there is no man who layeth it to heart*, Jer. xii. 11.

29, 15. *jaundice*, ictericia ; so called because it was supposed to be cured by the sight of the *icterus*, a bird mentioned by Pliny.

29, 23. *the two Lazaruses*, *cp.* Luke xvi. 20 ; John xi. 14, the one Lazarus suffering the corruption of disease, the other that of death.

30, 6. *cp.* Job ii. 8.

30, 15. *bondmen and bondwomen*, *cp.* Deut. xxviii. 68.

30, 19. *such terrors as might frighten even the brave ;* evidently suggested by a legal maxim which he found in Bracton, derived no doubt through Azo from the Digest :—" Debemus accipere metum non . . . vani vel meticulosi hominis sed talem qui cadere possit in virum constantem."

31, 22. *cp.* Martial i. 39.

> " Quem recitas, meus est, O Fidentine ! libellus ;
> Sed male quum recitas, incipit esse tuus."

32, 8. *Carmentis, cp.* Ch. VIII.

32, 11. *Bologna,* one of the great Universities.

32, 13. *treacherous copyists, cp.* Chaucer's verses to Adam Scrivener.

33, 3. *that which is against nature, cp.* Rom. i. 25–26.

33, 10. *sold our people for nought,* Ps. xliv. 12.

V

34. The title in the original is as follows :—" Querimonia librorum contra religiosos possessionatos," *i.e.* " possessioners," as contrasted with the mendicant friars.

34, 5. *between the hours of prayer,* " inter horas canonicas " ; the day was divided into eight periods of three hours, marked by as many acts of devotion.

34, 10. *full of cherubic letters,* " cherubicis libris plena," the reference is probably to the brilliant miniatures and ornamentations of old manuscripts ; perhaps only to the general beauty— " angelical."

34, 14. *Martha nor Mary* ; Martha and Mary were treated as types of the active and contemplative life ; similarly, Rachel and Leah. " Ubi nec meretur Martha corripi nec Maria" ; the old edd. read " corrumpi."

35, 11. *not bread baked in the ashes,* "panes non subcinericeos" ; *cp.* Ezek. iv. 12.

35, 20. *that we might catch the young foxes, cp.* Song of Songs, ii. 15.

36, 2. *the choice trappings of war-horses ;* " dextrariorum phaleræ præelectæ."

36, 6. *Liber Bacchus*, etc. ; " Liber Bacchus respicitur et in ventrem traicitur nocte dieque ; Liber codex despicitur et a manu reicitur longe lateque."

36, 17. *Timotheus*, the famous Greek musician : the reference may be from Boethius, *De Musica*, bk. 1.

37, 1. *the canons regular*, as opposed to "the canons secular" ; the former observed not only the " canones " or rules imposed upon all the clergy, but also the " regulæ " of St. Augustine.

37, 22. *like a sherd* ; " ut testa " ; *cp.* Ps. xxii. 15.

37, 22. *cp. Wisdom* xvii. 5.

VI

38, 1. *poor in spirit* ; *cp.* Matt. v. 3.

38, 2. *offscourings of the world*, "mundi peripsema," *cp.* 1 Cor. iv. 13.

38, 2. *salt of the earth*, *cp.* Matt. v. 13.

38, 3. *fishers of men*, *cp.* Matt. iv. 19.

38, 5. *to possess your souls in patience*, *cp.* Luke xxi. 19.

39, 1. *your sound may go forth*, *cp.* Ps. xix. 4.

39, 9. *to sow upon all waters*, *cp.* Isa. xxxii. 20.

39, 10. *no respecter of persons*, *cp.* Acts x. 34.

39, 10. *nor does the Most Holy desire the death of sinners*, *cp.* Ezek. xxxiii. 11.

39, 14. *in the spirit of lenity*, *cp.* Gal. vi. 1.

39, 16. *And having planted*, *cp.* 1 Cor. iii. 6.

39, 19. *the salvation of faithful souls*, *cp.* 1 Pet. i. 9.

39, 20. *the order of Preachers*, "fratres prædicantes," was instituted by St. Dominic, who obtained the Papal sanction from Honorius III. in 1216, on condition of adopting the Rule of St. Augustine.

40, 9. *the poor and neeay*, *cp.* Ps. xl. 17.

40, 21. *strange heresies*, "Hiberas nænias " ; the phrase comes from St. Jerome's preface to the Pentateuch, and orginally referred to certain Iberian, or Spanish, heresies.

41, 2. The reference is to St. Augustine's Epistles, cxxxvii.

42, 1. *if we speak according to human notions*, "si per anthropospatos (codd. ἀνθρωποπάθειαν) sermo fiat."

42, 3. *putting their hope*, *cp.* 2 Cor. iii. 12 ; x. 15.

42, 4. *the raven*, *cp.* Luke xii. 24, 27.

42, 13. *reliance*, "innisum," *cp.* Prov. iii. 5 ; the passage is corrupt in the MSS. and previous editions.

42, 20. *with summer fruit*, *cp.* Amos viii. 1.

43, 13. *against the law*, *cp.* Deut. xxii. 10.

43, 16. *the oxen were ploughing*, *cp.* Job i. 14.

43, 21. *the heap of Mercury* ; Mercury was the patron of merchants ; "acervus Mercurii" (the heap of Mercury) was used for counters ; the phrase here seems to mean "merely worthless counters."

43, 23. *blind watchman*, *cp.* Isa. lvi. 10.

44, 24. *he beats the air*, *cp.* 1 Cor. ix. 26.

45, 19. *with the cunning steward*, *cp.* Luke xvi. 3, 8.

VII

46, 2. *scatter the nations that delight in war*, *cp.* Ps. lxviii. 30.

46, 8. *Apollo becomes the Python's prey* ; in reference to the fight of Apollo and Python, the serpent produced from the mud left on the earth after the deluge of Deucalion ; it lived in the caves of Mount Parnassus, but was slain by Apollo, who founded the Pythian games in commemoration of his victory.

46, 8. *et tunc Phronesis pia mater in phrenesis redigitur potestatem.* "Phronesis," *i.e.* practical wisdom, prudence, "the virtue concerned in the government of men," is personified in Martianus Capella, *De Nuptiis Philologiæ et Mercurii*, as the mother of philology.

47, 2. *master of the master of the world* ; Aristotle was the tutor and adviser of Alexander the Great.

47, 5. *from his sacred home*, "a sacratis ædibus"; some MSS. read "Socratis." The reference has not been explained. *Sacratis ædibus* occurs in 2 Macc. vi. 4.

47, 9. *O most wicked power of darkness*, cp. Luke xxii. 53; Col. i. 13.

47, 10. *the approvea divinity of Plato*, "Platonis . . . deitatem probatam"; cp. *De disciplina Scholarium*, iv., "Platonis probata divinitas."

47, 13. *before form had put on its garb of matter*, "ante quam hylen entelechia induisset"; Arist. *Met.* xi. 8, 13 : τὸ τί ἦν εἶναι οὐκ ἔχει ὕλην τὸ πρῶτον· ἐντέλεχεια γάρ.

ἐντέλεχεια, the actual being of a thing; according to Aristotle, the soul is the ε. of the body, *that by which it actually is*, though it had a δύναμις or *capacity of existing* before.

This is the famous word which so puzzled Hermolaus Barbarus that he is said to have summoned the devil to his assistance.

47, 20. *to some rascal robber*, "vitiosi vispilionis"; *vispilio*, a robber; cp. the classical *vespillo*, a pauper's undertaker.

47, 21. *We bemoan Pythagoras*; the reference is to the death of Pythagoras in consequence of political disturbances at Crotona.

47, 23. *the wailings of a dove*, cp. Isa. lx. 8.

47, 24. *We mourn, too, for Zeno*; De Bury has confounded Zeno the Stoic, who died of old age, with Zeno of Elea, of whom the story mentioned in the text is told. The authorities vary the name of the tyrant. "Diomedon" (corrupted in the MSS. and texts) is from the version as told by Hermippus.

48, 11. *Cp. Aulus Gellius*, vi. 17. De Bury wrote "secundo bello Alexandrino"; Aulus Gellius, "bello priore Alexandrino"; the number varies in the MSS., but according to Gellius it was "millia ferme septinginta," hence the rendering in the text.

48, 21. *innocents in whose mouth was no guile*, cp. Rev. xiv. 5.

48, 25. *a pious daughter*; the text reads "filia virgo."

49, 3. *on his unyielding neck*, "collo irreflexo"; the phrase was derived from Boethius, *De Cons. Phil.* iv. metr. 7.

49, 4. *now for the second time*; the first time being when

poisoned by the shirt of Nessus, he ascended a pile of wood and ordered it to be set on fire.

49, 6. *Jonithus*; according to Methodius, a fourth son of Noah, who was supposed to have invented astronomy.

49, 8. *his brother Zoroaster*; *cp*. Gervase Tilbury, *Otia Imper*. i. 20. "Zoroaster alio nomine Cham filius Noæ vocabatur."

49. 9. *Enoch*; *cp*. Ecclus. xliv. 16.

49, 13. *caught up in an ecstasy*, *cp*. 2 Cor. xii. 4.

49, 16. *the book of the Perfect Word*; "liber Logostilios"; the reference is to the lost treatise of the quasi-mythical Hermes Trismegistus, extant only in the Latin translation of Apuleius, which was entitled Λόγος τέλειος, or, as St. Augustine renders it, *Verbum Perfectum*.

49, 17. *the older Athens*, *cp*. the *Timæus* and *Crito* of Plato, for the account of the Egyptian Athens supposed to be given to Solon by a priest of Sais.

50, 5. *Nay, Aristotle would not have missed*, etc. ; "Numquid Aristotelem de circuli quadratura syllogismus apodicticon latuisset."

51, 2. *like sheep*, *cp*. Ezek. xxxiv. 5.

51, 5. *the gates of death*; Ps. cvii. 18.

51, 8. *that translation of books*; the story is taken from Aulus Gellius, *Noctes Atticæ*, vi. 17.

51, 11. *O glad and joyful return*; "O postliminium gratiosum."

52, 3. *the Gades*; *i.e.* limit. Originally a Punic word meaning boundary, in which sense the place-name was used in mediæval Latin.

52, 5. *the ruler of Olympus*, "rector Olympi"; Ovid. *Met* ix. 498.

VIII

54, 22. *Aumbries*, "armaria"; "armarium" was a monastic term for a book-chest, hence also 'a library'; and the librarian was called "armarius" ("The Care of Books" by Mrs. J. W. Clark).

55, 6. *in purple and fine linen*, *cp.* Exod. xxxv. 6.

55, 7. *in sackcloth and ashes*, *cp.* Matt. xi. 21.

55. 8. *given up to oblivion*, *cp.* Ps. xxx. 13.

55, 11. *his stores of gums and spices*, "aromatum apothecas,' *cp.* Isa. xxxix. 2.

56, 1–4. "Sed revera libros non libras maluimus, codicesque plus dileximus quam florenos, ac panfletos exiguos incrassatis prætulimus palefridis." "Panfletos" appears to be one of the earliest recorded instances—if not the earliest instance—of the word.

57, 1. *the lounges of Athens.* "Athenarum diverticula."

57, 9. *Dionysius* the Areopagite, to whom were attributed a number of treatises, now believed to be the later productions of some Christian Neo-Platonists.

57, 10. *the Virgin Carmentis*, "Virgo Carmenta"; Cadmus the Phoenician is supposed to have introduced the alphabet into Greece, whence it was carried into Italy by Evander the Arcadian. His mother Carmenta accompanied him, and she is said to have turned the Greek into Roman characters.

57, 15. *cp.* Prov. xx. 14.

59, 14. *high schools*, "generalia studia."

59, 19. *nets and snares*, *cp.* Ezek. xii. 13.

60, 20. *all that is delicious*, *cp.* Wisdom xvi. 20.

61, 2. *cp.* Exod. xxxi. 4.

61, 4. *cp.* Exod. xxxv. 35.

61, 7. *cp.* Exod. xxvi. 1–7.

61, 8. *cp.* Exod. xxvi. 14.

61, 10. *oxen treading out corn*, *cp.* 1 Cor. ix. 9.

61, 11. *stars remaining*, *cp.* Judges v. 20.

61, 14. *cp.* Matt. xx. 6.

61, 24. *the preachers and Minors*, "prædicatores et minores," *cp.* Chap. VI.

62, 3. *tabulation*, "tabulationibus," possibly indexes or summaries.

62, 13. *stationers*, the "stationarii" of the Middle Ages were originally rather lenders than sellers of books.

62, 24. *with usury*, "cum usuris," *cp.* Luke xix. 23.

IX

66, 12. *Phocas*, one of the favourite grammars of the middle ages :—

> "Omnia cum veterum sint explorata libellis,
> Multa loqui breviter sit novitatis opus."

67, 3. *De Vetula*, erroneously assigned to Ovid ; the passage quoted run as follows :—

> "Omnes declinant ad ea, quæ lucra ministrant,
> Utque sciant discunt pauci, plures ut abundent ;
> Sic te prostituunt, O virgo Scientia ! sic te
> Venalem faciunt castis amplexibus aptam,
> Non te propter te quærentes, sed lucra per te,
> Ditarique volunt potius, quam philosophari.
> * * * *
> Sic Philosophia
> Exilium patitur, et Philopecunia regnat."

69, 23. *Peribermenias* ; the *De Interpretatione* of Aristotle ; called by this name in the Middle Ages.

70, 1. *with baneful haste and a harmful diploma*, "dispendioso compendio damnosoque diplomate."

70, 8. *papal provisions ;* the Statute of Provisors, 1350, was directed against this practice.

70, 11. *building up Sion in blood*, cp. Micah iii. 10.

71, 4. *and reacheth from end to end*, etc., cp. Wisdom, viii. 1.

71, 14. *so her soldiery are unmanned and languishing.* This was written a year or two before the battle of Creçy.

X

73, 12. *lynx-eyed*, "oculis lynceis" ; the phrase originally referred to Lynceus, the Argonaut, who was famed for the keenness of his vision ; then it was transferred to the lynx, and gave rise to the fable that it could see through a wall.

73, 24. *Pandects.* The term Pandects, from the Greek πανδέκται, was applied to encyclopedic works, and the term is used by Justinian in referring to the digest of Roman law made by his orders from the writings of the Roman jurists.

73, 25. *Tegni;* the writings of Galen were known in the Middle Ages through the Arabian physicians, and the title of his τέχνη Ἰατρική, his best known work, was corrupted into *Tegni* or *Tegne.*

74, 1. *Avicenna,* the famous Arabian philosopher and physician of the eleventh century, drew largely from the writings of the Greeks.

74, 2. *Almagest, cp.* Chap. I. 10. 6.

74, 17. *Parthenius,* a Greek poet, of whom a single line has come down to us in consequence of its adoption by Virgil into the Georgics (i. 437).

75, 17. *Mother of God,* "Theotokos." Nestorius, the Bishop of Constantinople, refused to apply the name Θεοτόκος to the Virgin Mary, and this heresy led to his deposition and to the separation of the Eastern and Western Churches. A great part of the life of S. Cyril, the bishop of Alexandria, was devoted to the contest with Nestorius, whose deposition at the Council of Ephesus he brought about in 431.

76, 16. *Clement V.* At the Council of Vienna in 1312, Raymond Lully obtained from the Council a decree for the establishment of professorships of Greek, Hebrew, Arabic, and Chaldee in Rome, Paris, Oxford, Bologna, and Salamanca, at the expense of the Pope and the prelates. Roger Bacon had urged Clement IV. to cause Greek, Hebrew and Arabic to be taught in the Universities. His Greek Grammar, together with a fragment of his Hebrew Grammar, has recently been edited by E. Nolan and S. A. Hirsch (Cambridge, 1902): these were perhaps the grammars referred to by De Bury (*cp.* also, "The Cambridge Modern History," vol. i., chapter xvii.).

XI

77, 4. *the children of this world,* "hujus sæculi filiis," *cp.* Luke xvi. 8.

78, 10. *the over-mastering love of books*, "librorum amor hereos"; nearly all the MSS. read *hereos*, one MS. *herous*, *ereus*. The word is one of the few unsettled cruces, if not the only crux, in the *Philobiblon*, and baffled even Mr. Thomas's efforts; he proposed δεινός, in view of the difficulty of *hereos*, "of which no trace is to be found in the dictionaries." But surely the MSS. are correct; "amor hereos" reminds one of Chaucer's phrase, "the loveres maladye of Hereos," *i.e.* the lover's disease of Eros (Knight's Tale, 515); amor hereos=love-passion, "hereos" being used in apposition to amor or adjectively.

78, 16. *the scorpion in treacle*, *cp*. Arist. Opp. Lat. 1496 f. 573 : "Hæc scientia utilis est, ut est utilis scorpio in tyriaca ; quæ licet sit toxicum tamen si datur patienti dolorem minuit et præstat remedium." The *De Pomo*, a treatise on the immortality of the soul, was falsely attributed to Aristotle, being really translated from the Hebrew by Manfred, son of the Emperor Frederick II.

79, 1. *cp*. Luke xi. 34–36.

79, 4. *for the regulation of social life*, *cp*. Wisdom viii. 9.

79. 6. *synteresis*, "a naturall power of ye soule, set in the highest part thereof, mooving and stirring it to good, and abhorring evil" (*the Doctor and Student*, dialog. 1. c. 13).

XII

82, 3. *royal roads*, "stratas regias."

XIII.

84, 18, 21. Horace, A.P. 333, 343 :—

"Aut prodesse volunt aut delectare poetæ. "

"Omne tulit punctum qui miscuit utile dulci. "

85, 1. *Pons Asinorum*, the original reads "elefuga," *cp*.

Roger Bacon, Op. Tert. ii. 21 : " Quinta propositio geometriæ Euclidis dicitur Elefuga, id est fuga miserorum."

85, 3. *cp.* John vi. 60.

85, 4. *The child of inconstancy* ; Mr. Thomas discovered the source of this passage in the *De disciplina scholarium*, a work long attributed to Boethius.

86, 7. Gratian collected the decrees and constitutions of the Popes into a body of canon law.

87, 3. *cp.* Donatus' life of Virgil, c. xviii.

XIV

88, 11. *Aristotle, cp.* Met. i. 2.

89, 1. *Sceptre in her left hand, cp.* De Cons. Phil. i. pr. 4.

89, 5. *cp.* the passage in the 5th Bk. of the *Republic*, cited by Boethius.

89, 20. *the charioteer of his father's car,* " currus auriga paterni," *cp.* Ovid, Met. ii. 327.

XV

91, 4. *Though one should speak, cp.* 1 Cor. xiii. 1.

91, 10. *cp.* Wisdom xvii. 18.

92, 6. *cp.* Ovid, Remed. Am. 139.

93, 4. *No iron-stained hand*, etc., from the *Eutheticus*, or ntroductory verses to the *Policraticon* of John of Salisbury :—

" Nulla libris erit apta manus ferrugine tincta,
    Nec nummata queunt corda vacare libris.
Non est ejusdem nummos librosque probrare ;
    Persequitur libros grex, Epicure, tuus.
Nummipetæ cum libricolis nequeunt simul esse ;
    Ambos, crede mihi, non tenet una domus."

93, 10. *Mammon, cp.* Matt. vi. 24.

93, 14. *The demon who derives his name ɟrom knowledge, cp.*

Aug. De Civ. Dei, ix. 20 : " Δαίμονες enim dicuntur, quoniam vocabulum graecum est, ob scientiam nominati."

94, 1. *cp.* Wisdom xiii. 5 ; Rom. i. 25.

94, 6. *Charity is not puffed up, cp.* I Cor. xiii. 4.

94, 19. *as well as those that are not, cp.* Rom. iv. 17.

95, 12. *which eye hath not seen, cp.* I Cor. ii. 9.

95, 15. *to separate substances,* probably the reference is to the angels.

96, 20. *cp.* Acts viii. 27.

XVI

98, 2. *arms,* " arma Vulcania."

99, 6. *seed to its dead brother, cp.* Deut. xxv. 5 ; Matt. xxii. 24.

99, 7. *cp.* Ecclus. xxx. 4.

99, 14. Cassiodorus, *De institutione divinarum litterarum,* Ch. 30.

100, 19. *cp.* Job xxxi. 35.

100, 22. *cp.* Jer. xxxvi. 18.

101, 5. *Being dead,* etc., *cp.* Heb. xi. 4.

101, 17. *the longevity of the ancients,* " polychronitudinem antiquorum," corrupted in some MSS. " ppolicritudinem," " policrotudinem," " pulcritudinem," " sollicitudinem."

101, 23. *cp.* Josephus, Antiq. Jud. i. 3, 9.

102, 3. *energy,* the better MSS. seem to point to the reading εὐεξία " euechia," rather than *energia.*

XVII

105, 20. *as black as jet,* " gagati simillimum."

106, 6. *wallet,* " eleemosynarium," i.e. alms-bag.

106, 15. *Now the rain is over and gone,* etc., *cp.* Song of Songs ii. 11, 12.

107, 11, 12. *the Latinist ana sophister ;* the students were enjoined to use Latin in ordinary conversation ; hence they might be called Latinistæ. In the third year of his residence the student of the liberal arts was allowed to become a " sophister," and to take part in logical disputations.

108, 1. *the clasps*, " signacula," *cp.* Rev. v. 2.

108, 11. *he who walketh without blemish*, *cp.* Ps. xv. 2.

XVIII

110, 7. *with singleness of eye*, "oculo simplici," *cp.* Matt. vi. 22.

107, 7. *the right hand*, etc., *cp.* Matt. vi. 3.

110, 8. *the lump is uncorrupted by leaven*, *cp.* 1 Cor. v. 6 ; *cp.* Gal. v. 9.

110, 9. *Nor is the garment woven of wool and linen*, *cp.* Deut. xxii. 11.

111, 9. *now for excess of curiosity*, " nunc de curiositate superflua," *cp.* 1 Tim. v. 13.

111, 14. *the heart and reins*, *cp.* Ps. vii. 9.

111, 19. *the ultimate springs of which they cannot see*, " quorum fontale non vident principium," *cp.* " virtutis et sapientiæ fontale principium," used of the University of Paris by the Cistercians in 1322.

112, 9. *the chief nursing mother*, etc., "omnium artium nutrice præcipua."

112, 22. *to the lovers of pelf*, " nummicolis."

113, 7. *under the aspect of Mercury*, *cp.* Roger Bacon, Op. Maj. p. 121. " Mercurius est significator scripturæ et scriptorum et profunditatis scientiarum."

XIX

114, 13. *in—Hall at Oxford*, the best MSS. read—N— ; probably for *Nomen*, signifying that some name was to be filled in. Most modern editors print *nostra*.

115, 7. *Five of the scholars*, " quinque de scholaribus," nearly equivalent to " Fellows."

XX

118, 7. *in the dust of vanity*, *cp.* Mic. i. 10.

118, 14. *unprofitable servants*, *cp.* Luke xvii. 10.

118, 15. *the most holy Job*, etc., *cp.* Job ix. 28.

119, 1. *as filthy rags*, *cp.* Isa. lxiv. 6.

119, 7. *as Dionysius*, *cp.* Op. cit. iv. 30 :—Συνελόντι δὲ φάναι τὸ ἀγαθὸν ἐκ τῆς μιᾶς καὶ τῆς ὅλης αἰτίας, τὸ δὲ κακὸν ἐκ πολλῶν καὶ μερικῶν ἐλλείψεων.

120, 13. *our spirit may desire to be dissolved*, *cp.* Phil. i. 23.

120, 15. *our conversation may be in Heaven*, *cp.* Phil. iii. 20.

120, 18. *returning from the husks*, *cp.* Luke xv. 16–17.

120, 19. *the piece of silver that has been lately found*, *cp.* Luke xv. 8–9.

120, 23. *that old serpent*, *cp.* Rev. xii. 9.

121, 1. *the awful judgment-seat*, "terrendum tribunal," *cp.* 2 Cor. v. 10–11.

121, 5. *the frame of our carnal nature*, "carnalis naturæ figmentum," *cp.* Ps. ciii. 14.

121, 19. *the bottomless pit*, *cp.* Rev. xx. 3.

121, 21. *the most deserving Confessor Cuthbert*, St. Cuthbert, the patron Saint of the Cathedral at Durham, Bishop of Lindisfarne in 685 ; his final resting-place became the seat of the Palatine See.

122, 1. *his assessor*, "concessorem," *cp.* Eph. ii. 6, "consedere fecit in cælestibus" ; other MSS. and texts "confessorem."